NOV 17

THE
CHURCH

THE
CHURCH

Unlocking the Secrets to the Places
Catholics Call Home

Cardinal Donald Wuerl
and Mike Aquilina

IMAGE

New York

IMAGE is a registered trademark, and the "I" colophon is a trademark of Random House, Inc.

Library of Congress Cataloging-in-Publication Data
Wuerl, Donald W.
The church: unlocking the secrets to the places Catholics call home / Donald Wuerl and Mike Aquilina.—1st ed.
1. Catholic church buildings.   2. Catholic Church—Liturgical objects.
3. Church decoration and ornament.   I. Aquilina, Mike.   II. Title.
BX1970.3.W84 2013
246'.9582—dc23   2012031467

ISBN 978-0-7704-3551-6
eISBN 978-0-7704-3552-3

PRINTED IN THE UNITED STATES OF AMERICA

Photos show the Cathedral of Saint Matthew the Apostle and the Church of Saint Stephen Martyr, both in Washington, D.C. All photos by Paul Fetters.

Jacket design by Laura Duffy
Jacket photograph by Brian Moran

10 9 8 7 6 5 4 3 2 1

First Edition

CONTENTS

CONTENTS

THE
CHURCH

Foreword

By Cardinal Daniel DiNardo

In the course of reading *The Church: Unlocking the Secrets to the Places Catholics Call Home,* certain passages took me back to a time in my seminary days, during my theological studies in Rome, when I had the opportunity to focus

on my advanced degree in Patristics, the study of the early
Fathers of the Church. The basilicas of Rome that are so
prevalent to the landscape of that ancient city have never
been of mere historical or archaeological interest to me.
The beauty of the stones, the timeless architecture, and the
edifying liturgical furnishings of those ancient churches
are living reminders of the early Church Fathers, some
of whom, such as Saint Jerome and Saint Leo the Great,
celebrated the Divine Liturgy within those very walls.
Others, like Saint Polycarp of Smyrna and Hippolytus,
visited Rome at a time before there were many Christian
churches. And some bravely offered their blood in martyrdom on the ground of the Eternal City as did the very
early Church Father, Saint Ignatius of Antioch.

The Fathers of the Church wrote about the Church as
God's Holy Mystery and Sacrament, sometimes describing the Church as a living Temple, as the Mother of the
Faithful, and as a beautiful vine. They never lost the intimate connection and unity of the Church as the *Christus
Totus,* the whole Christ, both Head and members, and the
church building as a place set aside as a space of beauty for
the sanctification of God's holy people. Particularly memorable is Saint Ambrose's wondrous description for newly
baptized Christians about what transpired on the holy
night of the Easter Vigil when they were washed clean
and illuminated, sealed with the chrism of Confirmation,
and, with awe, celebrated the Eucharist in full for the first
time. The Church Fathers also passed on to us their commentary on the beauty of the altar, the ambo and the baptistery, the places where the Church was being continually

born, instructed, and nourished; the places where the Sacrifice of the Lord was being celebrated. Saint Ambrose's reflection on the significance of the baptistery and the altar I found to be eloquent and inspired.

The ancient Fathers of East and West are indeed the original "tour guides" and experts on the meaning of our church buildings, their furnishings and iconography. Their reflections on the relics of the martyrs over whose tombs altars were erected; their praise of the mosaics and frescoes of Christ, the Blessed Virgin Mary, and the saints; and their astute observations on how the floral and "nature" designs on the walls and floors of the church echo something of the beauty of nature and creation that inevitably points us to the greater beauty that dwells within our Creator, the Lord of all—all of these meditations are an excellent way to get to the "heart" of who and what the Church is and why her buildings are so instructive to us about our Catholic faith.

Throughout the centuries, the meaning of Church buildings, of Church architecture, and of their decoration has continued to develop in every part of the world. There are beautiful examples of churches great and small in our own country, from those erected a few centuries ago up to those built during our own lifetimes. Many of them, in the eyes of the informed, bear the marks and possess the same symbols and meaning as those churches praised by the Church Fathers.

Cardinal Wuerl and Mike Aquilina previously collaborated on a book about the Mass. This present publication is a most informative and insightful investigation of

the meaning of the church building itself. Through their analysis, one also discovers (or rediscovers, as the case may be) the meaning of who we are as the Catholic Church. I am pleased, prejudicially of course, that so many of my "friends" in the Patristic period are cited and explored in the book. In a fresh and interesting way, this book opens us again to the meaning of *mystagogy,* that beautiful Patristic way of using the places and spaces of our buildings to draw us deeper into the experience of Sacred Scripture and the sacraments, the understanding of our Catholic faith, and the beauty and wonder of holiness in which the Holy Trinity dwells and in Whose life we are invited to share. This book helps us to open our eyes and be initiated, through the visible mysteries of sacraments and the signs that the sacraments "use," into the invisible realities they signify and make present and real.

    This book is a fine example of a *porta fidei,* a "door of faith," that opens us into what is our present and final goal, the great Supper of the Lamb magnificently described in the final pages of the final book of the Holy Scriptures, the book of Revelation. It serves as an invitation to revisit and experience anew the mystery of the heart of the Church when we find ourselves immersed in the pages of *The Church: Unlocking the Secrets to the Places Catholics Call Home.*

Preface

By Father Robert Barron

Centuries ago, even very ordinary believers knew how to "read" a church. That is to say, they could decipher the meaning embedded in the art, the stained glass, the sanctuary furnishings, and the sculpture within a church building. In the years following the Second Vatican Council, I'm afraid that most Catholics lost this knack. This was due not to the texts of the Council themselves, but to certain trends within contemporary architecture and spirituality that influenced the construction of churches during the last fifty years. Modernist architectural theory dictated that buildings should be reduced to their essential characteristics, their bare bones. This led to churches that were sleek, streamlined, functional. And many theologians and spiritual writers of the last half-century so emphasized the fact that *church* means the people of God that they understressed the symbolic and spiritual power of ecclesial

buildings themselves. As one very seminal document from the 1970s put it, the church structure is simply "the skin of the worshipping assembly," a kind of tent that shelters the congregation for a time, only to be struck as the pilgrim people move on. The result of these two influences was "beige" churches, largely empty "gathering spaces," devoid of color, symbolism, and artistic texture.

The very serious problem with these modernist churches is that they violated the principle that Blessed John Henry Newman identified as absolutely fundamental to the Catholic sensibility, namely, the incarnational principle. The Word became flesh and dwelt among us, and this means that God is pleased to express himself precisely through very physical stuff—color, painting, sculpture, architecture, and so forth. Occasionally in the history of Christianity, the puritanical, iconoclastic idea has arisen, but the Catholic Church has always opposed it. And that is precisely why we have Hagia Sophia, Chartres Cathedral, the Sainte-Chapelle, the Sistine Chapel, and the Basilica of the National Shrine of the Immaculate Conception. Those magnificent structures are themselves sacramental, bearers of the sacred.

In this wonderful book, Cardinal Donald Wuerl and Mike Aquilina have performed the signal service of reminding us of the incarnational principle as it is embodied in churches. Like good and patient teachers, they have instructed us again how to read Christ's presence in the dense textures of our cathedrals, basilicas, chapels, and churches. For example, they tell us how the cruciform design of most classical ecclesial buildings is meant to invoke the human body itself, but more precisely that particular human body that was nailed to a cross two millennia ago. They also show how something as ordinary as the chair in which the presider sits is actually charged with meaning, for it speaks of the teaching authority that the priest has derived from his bishop, who in turn derived it from the Apostles and hence from Christ himself. One of the most illuminating (pun intended) sections for me had to do with stained glass. The authors show how the figures depicted in the painted glass are never meant to look "realistic," that is, ordinary and of this world. Instead, they are meant to be idealized, for they represent the saints who dwell now in the fullness of glory, in the inaccessible light of heaven.

Savor this small but very informative book. Use it as an occasion for prayer and meditation. Bring it into a classical church with you as an interpretive key. And then pass it on to someone who could benefit from it, perhaps especially to a person who came of age during the era of beige churches.

A Note About Our Approach

We, the authors, are Catholics of the Latin Rite, so we are heirs to a certain distinctive tradition of building, decoration, and liturgical prayer, and that tradition is reflected in the pages of this book.

The tradition is vast enough to accommodate many styles of art and architecture, from Romanesque to rococo, from Gothic to Mission. This book, however, is not about architecture, but rather about the elements most commonly found in the churches of our particular tradition. The Christian Church is catholic, which means "universal," and other cultures have produced other ritual families with their own distinct traditions of church architecture and decoration. We will touch on some of these, but only briefly and in passing. This book is, in the main, about the churches we have known in the tradition we know best. We intend this book as a guide to the Catholic churches most commonly encountered by ordinary readers in the Americas, where we live.

Throughout the book we have capitalized *Church* when we are referring to the one, holy, catholic, and apostolic body of believers. We have lowercased *church* when it refers to the building in which such believers worship.

We approach our subject from two distinct viewpoints. One of us is a cardinal-archbishop, an ordained priest of the Catholic Church, who has offered Mass at the altar for forty-six years. The other is a married layman, who has prayed with his family in the pews of hundreds of churches and tried to see the arches and vaults, ceilings and cloisters through his children's eyes. Working together we hope to share a panoramic vision of our churches.

This book is not a work of criticism. In aesthetic matters, we have our opinions and preferences, but this is not a book about our opinions and preferences. When we find ourselves in the presence of the living God—as we do whenever we go to church—we believe the proper response is not to play the critic and complain about decorations. The proper response is worship.

There are many good books about how to "read" a church. Catholics have been writing such works since at least the third century. To explain the history, meaning, symbolism, and scriptural foundations for the many parts that make up a church, this book will draw from the works of authors, from Eusebius and Maximus the Confessor to William Durand and Joseph Ratzinger. Our primary doctrinal sources are the official documents of the Church, especially the *Catechism of the Catholic Church* (hereafter abbreviated CCC), the *General Instruction of the Roman Missal* (GIRM), and the *Code of Canon Law* (CIC).

We want this book to be something more than a guidebook to ancient structures and furniture. If we help you to *read* a church, we do it with the hope that you'll be better able to *pray* a church. If you want to understand a church, you need to read it as a prayer book and not as an architecture textbook.

When you open a prayer book, you find *prayers* that should lead you to *prayer.* You find the words of the saints that should inspire you to raise your mind and heart to heaven and ask good things of God—but using your own words, or perhaps no words at all.

In a similar way, when you enter a church, you'll encounter many objects whose artists, artisans, and builders intended to inspire you to pray. Again, the more adept you are at "reading" their work—understanding their visual vocabulary—the better you'll be able to *pray* their churches. You'll see churches as they were built to be seen.

And that is really the most satisfying way to experience churches. For churches are not museums or merely tourist attractions. They are temples of the living God who wills and wishes to meet you there.

We have conceived this book to be a companion volume to our earlier book, *The Mass: The Glory, the Mystery, the*

Tradition. The two complement each other. In our earlier volume we discussed the vessels and vestments related to service at the altar. We have chosen not to cover the same material in this book. If you enjoy *The Church,* we hope you'll decide to read *The Mass* as well. If you've already read *The Mass,* we're pleased to have you back.

LOVE IS THE BUILDER

CATHOLICS LOVE their churches. We build them with love. We make them lovable.

If you visit a remote village in Latin America, the people will be pleased to show you *their* church—the church that they or their ancestors have raised to the glory of God. Step inside and you'll find a sanctuary adorned with precious items: skillfully wrought woodwork, stonework, and metalwork, and paintings and statues in the local style. If you linger for Mass, you'll see a chalice and plate of gold or silver, enhanced perhaps by gems.

The inside of the church may be lavish and rich, while the homes outside are simple and unadorned. And that contrast sometimes shocks people who are visiting from more prosperous lands. It has become a cliché of anti-Catholic prejudice to say that such precious objects would serve a better purpose if they were sold to raise money for food.

The people in the village know better. They know that the money earned from such a sale would feed them for no more than a few days, while the loss would leave them impoverished forever. Without their church—*their* church—they would be spiritually and culturally destitute. For they've built and furnished their church with love, as Catholics everywhere do and always have done.

Such love finds expression in the smallest details of construction and decoration, and in a seemingly infinite variety of styles. You'll see it in Ethiopia's ancient churches—carved out of a single massive block of black stone, the size of a small mountain. You'll see it in Cappadocia's cave churches—occupied during a time when Christianity was illegal and the faith was forced underground (literally). You'll see it in the play of dark and light in the Gothic cathedrals of the Middle Ages. You'll find

it in the most ordinary suburban churches in the United States.

These churches, in all their diversity, are built according to a common plan, furnished with similar items, and decorated with remarkably standard symbols, scenes, and images. The elements bespeak a love shared by Catholics from all over the world, regardless of language, culture, wealth, or historical period.

Catholics build their churches with love; and our love has a language all its own. Like romance, Christian devotion follows certain customs and conventions—a tradition poetic and courtly—hallowed by millennia of experience.

This book is about that silent language of love. In these pages we'll examine the structure of a church and its furnishings. We'll consider the historical and biblical roots of each element in a church, providing basic definitions, and we'll explain each element's meaning in the Christian tradition. Why, for example, do churches have spires and bells? Where did we get the custom of using holy water? How does an altar differ from an ordinary table? What are votive candles for?

Every part of a church is rich in meaning and mystery, theology and history. Every furnishing or ornament reveals some important detail of the story of our salvation. Through two millennia, Christians have preserved and developed a tradition of building and decoration. The tradition is supple enough that it could be adapted by local cultures as the Gospel spread to new lands, yet solid enough to protect and preserve the essential heritage received from the Apostles and revealed by God.

If you were making a movie and you wanted your audience to identify an interior immediately as a Catholic church, what would you do? You'd show sunlight streaming through stained glass. You'd angle your camera heavenward, looking upward past monumental statues of the saints. You'd pan across a bank of red votive candles with flickering flames, and then focus on an array of seemingly surreal images: a human heart surrounded by thorns; an eye; a disembodied hand raised in blessing; a painting of a woman standing on a crescent moon; a carving of a dove descending; a lion, an eagle, and an ox, all crowned by similar halos; and a throng of angels.

In the popular imagination, these elements add up to a Catholic *identity*. But what exactly does each of them mean?

And how do all the elements work together? What's the sense of the symbols? What are we trying to say through the medium of human body parts and exotic animals? Late in the fourth century Saint Augustine, who would go on to become a builder of churches, wrote: "I know that a truth which the mind understands in just one way can be materially expressed by many different means, and I also know that there are many different ways in which the mind can understand an idea that is outwardly expressed in one way."[1]

The African saint gives us an important insight for "reading" our churches: One image can convey many layers of meaning, and the same idea can be expressed in manifold ways.

Everything we see in a Catholic church is there for a single purpose: to tell a love story. It is a story as old as the world, and it involves the whole of creation, the

vast expanse of history, and every human being who ever
lived. It involves Almighty God, and it involves you.

Art and architecture are means of communication. Our churches speak of something remote, beyond
the reach of human sciences—what Dante called "the
Love that moves the sun and the other stars."[2] But our
churches speak also to something deep inside us—in our
souls and in our senses—because, as Dante added, the
same Love that moves the cosmos also moves "*my* desire
and *my* will."

To understand our churches is to begin to understand a
love at once unmistakably divine and profoundly human,
faraway and yet intimate. When we begin to understand
that love, it begins to light up our view of our churches
and their symbols.

The love story appears in compressed, poetic form in
the Gospel according to Saint John.

> In the beginning was the Word, and the Word
> was with God, and the Word was God. He was
> in the beginning with God; all things were made
> through him, and without him was not anything
> made that was made. In him was life, and the life
> was the light of men. The light shines in the dark-
> ness, and the darkness has not overcome it. . . .
>
> The true light that enlightens every man was
> coming into the world. He was in the world, and
> the world was made through him, yet the world
> knew him not. He came to his own home, and
> his own people received him not. But to all who

received him, who believed in his name, he gave power to become children of God; who were born, not of blood nor of the will of the flesh nor of the will of man, but of God.

And the Word became flesh and dwelt among

us, full of grace and truth; we have beheld his
glory, glory as of the only-begotten Son from the
Father. . . .

For God so loved the world that he gave his
only-begotten Son, that whoever believes in him
should not perish but have eternal life. (John 1:1–
5, 9–14; 3:16)

John begins his Gospel by describing a God of awesome power, remote in space and transcending time: a
Spirit, a Word. This is the God whom even the pagan
philosophers knew: the Prime Mover, the One. Yet, precisely where the pagan philosophers stalled, John's drama
proceeds to a remarkable climax: "And the Word became
flesh and dwelt among us."

From beyond the distant heavens, existing before the
beginning of time, God himself broke into history, took
on flesh, and made his dwelling—literally, "pitched his
tent"—among his people. Yes, God is eternally the Word,
but a word is elusive, and not everyone may grasp it.

God, who reigns in heaven, and who transcends all
creation and all time, assumed the life of an ordinary laborer, who could be seen and heard and touched. God
transformed all creation by his healing touch. He took up
residence among his people.

The early Christians said that when Jesus descended
into the river Jordan he sanctified—made holy—all the
waters of the earth, commissioning them for the task of
baptism. In his mother's womb he sanctified motherhood.
At a family table, God handled ordinary food and made it

to signify an otherwise unimaginable heavenly banquet. He wandered in the desert and traveled in boats and visited towns and cities. In doing all this, he blessed creation and hallowed it as a sign of his own eternal life.

Every Catholic church is built to tell this story, the story of how "God so loved the world." Every church is built to dispense the life-giving water and magnify the light that shines in the darkness. Every church serves the heavenly banquet at its family table: the altar. Every church is built as a memorial of God's sojourn among his people—and of his people's rejection of him. Front and center we keep the crucifix.

Our churches tell a love story, and they bring us salvation, and so we love them all the more. So much of Catholic identity is built into the houses we build for worship. Everything about our churches, inside and out, is a unique material token of the most profound spiritual love. Jesus has spiritualized the world, but he has done it by putting flesh on pure Spirit. That reality is reflected on the walls of every Catholic church.

Saint John of Damascus, writing in eighth-century Syria, pondered the things in his church and was moved, he said, to "worship the God of matter, who became matter for my sake, and willed to make his dwelling in matter, and who worked out my salvation through matter. I will not cease from honoring the matter that works my salvation. . . . Through matter, filled with divine power and grace, my salvation has come to me."[3]

Theologians call this the "sacramental principle."

Other authors, speaking colloquially, refer to it simply as "the Catholic Thing." That's how closely a Catholic's spiritual identity is tied to these material realities.

The sacramental principle tells us that, since the Word became flesh, God has begun to heal and restore his creation. Spiritual light can now shine through the material world. Because of the touch of Jesus Christ, matter can now convey God's grace. On one level, bread and wine; on another, oil, candles, fabrics and paint, bricks, blocks, and filigree—all these can mediate God's presence in the world.

Jesus's disciples, still today, can sense the dramatic effects of the Incarnation. With the poet Gerard Manley Hopkins we can look upon a world "charged with the grandeur of God"—and we can reflect that grandeur through the material objects and symbols present in our churches.

Reflecting God's grandeur is something we are drawn to do. It fulfills a need we have as Christians who have been redeemed. We want to praise and thank the Lord who has saved us. But it also fulfills a basic need we have as *human beings*; for the God who redeemed us is the God who created us, and he designed us to love beauty, to find delight in it, and to make beautiful things that tell us of the greater beauty of divine glory.

Christians need churches. It is said that for centuries the Benedictine order forbade the founding of a new monastery until the group of founders included a monk who could make bricks—and another who was trained in turning those bricks into church walls, raised according to the ancient models. From generation to generation they passed on the tradition of beauty, love, and wisdom that they had received, a tradition that libraries could not contain, yet one that we'll try to survey with you in the chapters that follow.

WHAT IS A CHURCH?

BEFORE HE was the Deliverer or the Lawgiver, Moses was a visionary. His first encounter with God happened while he was leading the flock of his father-in-law through the wilderness. When he came to Horeb, which was known as "God's mountain," the angel of the Lord appeared to him in the flames of a bush that was burning yet was not consumed by the fire. Moses stepped forward to explore the curiosity. From the fire, God called him by name. "Here am I!" Moses said. And the Lord told him: "Do not come near; put off your shoes from your feet, for the place on which you are standing is holy ground." Moses did as he was told, and the voice from the bush identified himself: "I am the God of your father, the God of Abraham, the God of Isaac, and the God of Jacob." Moses hid his face, we are told, because he was afraid to look at God (Exodus 3:1–6).

Moses found himself on "holy ground," and the realization filled him with a holy fear, a sense of awe.

A Catholic church is, by definition, "holy ground." The official documents define a church as "a sacred building designated for divine worship" (CIC 1214). Mount Horeb was sacred because of the special presence of God, and that same presence is what makes a Catholic church sacred. God is present there.

A church does not need to be a great work of art in order to be a sacred place. The philosopher Josef Pieper said: "A building does not become a church by virtue of its architecture, but by virtue of its consecration."[1] Some churches indeed are masterpieces, but even they are not "art for art's sake." A church is a building with a useful purpose. Like a firehouse or a hospital, it provides a *public service.* That's the root meaning of the word *liturgy,* which Christians use to denote their official worship. Catholic liturgy is a public service conducted in a public building. The religious law governing churches demands that parishioners be able to enter freely for prayer and worship, especially during sacred celebrations (CIC 1214 and 1221). Thus, a church's form must accommodate its ritual function—or the church will be judged a failure.

This may seem contradictory—for a church to be a "public building" and yet at the same time a "sacred place." But remember that "the Word became flesh and dwelt among us." It is in the church that the God-man takes his place among his people in every time and place.

The church is the holy ground where the divine Word is "made flesh" in the act that is most central to Catholic life: the sacrifice of the altar, the Holy Mass.

A church is built for the sake of the altar inside. The altar is built for the sake of the Mass. And the Mass is offered for the glory of God and for the salvation of his people.

Jesus himself set this order in place. On the night he was handed over to his persecutors, he shared his Last Supper with his Apostles. It was a solemn ritual meal, recognizably in the Jewish tradition, yet it also represented something new. For Jesus took bread, broke it, and said: "This is my body." Then he blessed a cup of wine and pronounced it to be "the cup of my blood." As he shared these with his Apostles, he gave them a clear instruction: "Do this in remembrance of me" (Luke 22:19–20).

His claim seems incredible: that bread could be his body and wine his blood. Yet he couldn't have stated it in simpler declarative sentences. Elsewhere he had explained, at great length: "I am the living bread which came down from heaven; if any one eats of this bread, he will live for ever; and the bread which I shall give for the life of the world is my flesh. . . . For my flesh is food indeed, and my blood is drink indeed. He who eats my flesh and drinks my blood abides in me, and I in him" (John 6:51, 55–56).

Then his command was as clear as his declaration. He instructed his Apostles to "do this"; and ever since then the Mass has been what Catholics do. It is the action, the event, that defines believers as Catholic. We see this in the very first generation of Christians. In the Acts of the Apostles we find the company of believers meeting in homes for "the Apostles' teaching and fellowship, to the breaking of the bread and to the prayers" (Acts 2:42). For the Catholic Christian, then as now, those actions add up to the Holy Mass.

The Mass is what we do, and we "do this" because Christ commanded that we do it (Luke 22). The *church* is the ordinary place where Catholics fulfill this obligation, and every Catholic church has been consecrated specifically for that purpose.

In the beginning, Christians worshipped wherever they could, usually in family homes (see Acts 2:46, Romans 16:5, Colossians 4:15, Philemon 2). As their numbers grew, they required larger spaces for worship, and wealthy converts sometimes turned over sizable properties to be set apart exclusively for worship and the everyday life of the community.

These "house churches" would be further expanded as the need arose, and many of them eventually became imposing buildings. A few have survived to the present day. Others have emerged from the sands through the good work of archaeologists. The third-century church in Dura-Europos, in Syria, for example, shows evidence that it was a family home expanded to serve the needs of local Christians. Eventually, it became a dedicated church, with walls lavishly decorated with biblical scenes as well as the sort of symbols still seen in churches today. In Rome several churches (most famously San Clemente) show signs of similar development. Most of the early house churches, unfortunately, were destroyed in the on-and-off persecutions of those early centuries.

Christians worshipped where they could—which meant that they adapted secular buildings, with their traditional plans, to the community's needs. In terms of interior decoration, Christians often followed the model of ancient Jewish synagogues, which in turn mimicked the layout of the Temple in Jerusalem. (We'll treat that topic in greater detail in a later chapter.)

The archaeologist Jerome Murphy-O'Connor has excavated many ancient sites, and he offers us an evocative reconstruction of the "family-type atmosphere at the liturgical celebrations."

> In winter it must have been rather cozy. The shutters were closed against the biting winds from the north, and a brazier gave both light and warmth. It was different in summer. The shutters could not be left open without attracting the unwelcome attention of the street. The flickering flames of oil lamps intensified the heat of the airless, crowded room. Such discomfort, however, meant little to those whose sharing of bread and wine brought Christ into their midst. As they in their poverty contemplated Jesus in his ultimate self-sacrifice, they were strengthened by the knowledge that the power of God is made perfect in weakness (2 Corinthians 12:9).[2]

The pattern continued even as Christianity became legal, in the early fourth century. Christians still worshipped where they could, but now they had free access to the best materials and properties that wealthy Christian families had to offer. The emperor Constantine turned over vast estates for use as churches. The main buildings were called basilicas—from the Greek word for king, *basileia*. They were constructed to be the monarch's "great halls," where he held court and received embassies. They followed a certain pattern—typically large, long colonnaded buildings—designed to impress visitors. Their size was symbolic of the king's power. Now they were adapted for use by the King of Kings, Jesus, for the rite he established as his memorial: the Mass.

These great halls in Rome were soon dedicated to the memory of the Apostles. The Lateran Palace became a church dedicated to Jesus the Savior and the two Saint Johns, the Baptist and the Evangelist. On Vatican Hill a grand basilica was constructed to honor Saint Peter, the Prince of the Apostles and the first pope. St. Peter in Chains was built over the location of an even earlier church dedicated to this Apostle. Outside the walls there was a basilica over the tomb of the Apostle Paul, and then another to the martyr Saint Agnes, and then many others.

The Roman inventory records show that Christians spared no expense in decorating the "great halls" of the King of Kings. To the Basilica of St. John Lateran, the emperor Constantine donated "a ciborium of hammered silver," which depicted Jesus enthroned. It was five feet tall and weighed 120 pounds. There were statues of the twelve

Apostles, and of four angels, also in silver, also weighing over a hundred pounds. The silver angels had jewels for eyes. Hundreds of lamps and dozens of chandeliers, all made of gold and silver, lit up the church's interior. The altars were made of silver, the altar plate of gold.

Over time, many different types of buildings were adapted for use as churches: marketplaces, military barracks, and administrative offices. These were modified, and other buildings were raised from the ground up, all to suit the same purpose: the gathering of the community for the celebration of the Mass.

The church is a public building that serves a useful purpose, yet it is also different from other buildings that are merely utilitarian or simply monuments of culture. A hundred pounds of silver in chandeliers may delight the eye as it reflects the candlelight, but its purpose is more than usefulness. Its purpose is glory.

Because a church is consecrated, it is set apart as something sacred, different from other structures, reserved for special use. It is built with the permission of a bishop, blessed by him, and operated under his authority (delegated, ordinarily, to a priest serving as pastor).

Faithful to their tradition, Christians give their best to ornament their churches. It is no exaggeration to say that most of the most beautiful works of architecture are works that have been dedicated to worshipping God: St. Peter's Basilica and the Sistine Chapel in Rome, Hagia Sophia in Istanbul, the Cathedral of Notre Dame de Chartres.

A church's function—to be a house of worship and prayer—inspires people to new and better forms. Prayer, according to a classic definition, is the raising of the mind and heart to God. If a church is beautiful, it elevates the sensibilities of the people who pray there. It raises their minds and hearts heavenward. A beautiful church can do a lot of the heavy lifting for struggling Christians as they pray.

Everything inside a church must serve this purpose. Canon law states: "Only those things which serve the exercise or promotion of worship, piety, or religion are permitted in a sacred place; anything not consonant with the holiness of the place is forbidden" (CIC 1210).

The things that are inside a church should be of the best quality. The great guidebook for those who celebrate the Mass is the *General Instruction of the Roman Missal,* and among its directives we read: "sacred buildings and requisites for divine worship should be truly worthy and beautiful and be signs and symbols of heavenly realities" (GIRM 288).

The same idea rings out in the *Catechism,* which defines a church as " 'a house of prayer in which the Eucharist is celebrated and reserved, where the faithful assemble, and where is worshipped the presence of the Son of God our Savior, offered for us on the sacrificial altar for the help and consolation of the faithful.' " This definition has consequences for the decoration we encounter in churches. The *Catechism* goes on to conclude: " 'This house ought to be in good taste and a worthy place for prayer and sacred ceremonial.' In this 'house of God' the truth and the harmony of the signs that make it up should show Christ to be present and active in this place" (CCC 1181).

Because Jesus Christ is really present in the Eucharist, Christians build churches with the greatest possible reverence. The blessing is a solemn ritual event. There, in the church, Catholics will eat the Body of Christ, as he himself instructed them to do, and thus become the Body of Christ. As Saint Paul put it in one of the earliest Christian documents: "The bread which we break, is it not a participation in the body of Christ? Because there is one bread, we who are many are one body, for we all partake of the one bread" (1 Corinthians 10:16–17).

The Eucharist is the greatest of the sacraments, the special signs that Christ entrusted to the Apostles as means of grace. But it is not the only sacrament. A church contains a baptismal font, for the initiation of new members, and confessionals, where sins are forgiven by the power of God. It is built with a cabinet, called the ambry, that houses the sacred oils used for anointing the sick and for administering the sacrament of confirmation.

The noble purpose of a church building has provoked the greatest geniuses to their highest aspirations.

Michelangelo was seventy-one years old when, in 1546, he was appointed architect for the rebuilding of St. Peter's Basilica in Rome. It was, in effect, a sentence of hard labor, and it could not be completed in his lifetime. Yet he took up the project eagerly and worked at it obsessively for the remainder of his days. The task of designing the great dome of the world's largest church, and supervising its construction, consumed Michelangelo's attention until his death, just shy of his eighty-ninth birthday. Every time the appreciative Pope Paul III tried to send money, it is reported that Michelangelo sent it back. Through a decade and a half, the artist insisted that he was to receive no payment for his labors but would do his duty "for the love of God."

A thousand years before Michelangelo, the emperor Justinian commanded the reconstruction of the great church of Hagia Sophia (Holy Wisdom) in his capital, Constantinople. In 537, when the church was almost complete, he stepped inside to see the work that had been done by the hands of ten thousand laborers.

Nothing in his experience could have prepared him for that moment. A church so massive should have been dark inside, but Hagia Sophia was luminous.

Justinian surveyed walls fifteen stories high made of marble and porphyry, and stone blocks of black and yellow and green, walls adorned with rare gems and sheets of precious metals. The emperor gazed into stone colonnades set row upon row. Upward he saw a beautiful and ingenious massive dome supported by half domes, each lined with mosaics of gold. The gold reflected light from galleries of windows and magnified it seemingly a millionfold. The interior appeared as radiant as a hilltop on the brightest spring day.

The emperor looked up at a mosaic image of Solomon, the Old Testament king who had built Jerusalem's mighty

Temple. Then he laughed with joy and exclaimed: *"Glory to God,* who has found me worthy to finish so great a work! Solomon, I have outdone you!" Justinian, like Michelangelo, created a masterpiece for the love of God.

Such accomplishments are not just part of ancient history. In Pittsburgh, in the twentieth century, steelworkers would finish their shift at the mills and then report for a full shift, unpaid, working on construction crews to build their magnificent parish churches. Such devotion could raise a grand basilica from the most improbable urban hillside. In Washington, D.C., the Basilica of the National Shrine of the Immaculate Conception arose thanks to the contributions of many thousands of the faithful, young and old alike.

Textbooks record history as if the most important figures were generals and kings and great artists like Michelangelo. This side of heaven, no one knows for sure. But the movers and shakers of history may be neither the emperors who pay for the churches nor the artists who make them beautiful, but rather the ordinary people who pray in the churches. The greatest accomplishments of Justinian and Michelangelo may be the prayers their works inspired.

No matter how grand the building, no matter how beautiful the art, churches are made to serve something infinitely greater. The church and its art are subordinate to the Real Presence they contain and adorn. A church is holy ground because of that presence.

WHAT IS *THE* CHURCH?

The English word *church* has ancient and beautiful origins. It comes from the Greek word *Kyriaké,* which means simply "the Lord's"—"belonging to the Lord."

What is it, exactly, that belongs to the Lord?

In English (and in many other languages), *church* has come to have two meanings. It describes the whole assembly of God's people: the Catholic Church. Yet it also denotes the parish building where those people worship: St. Stanislaus Church in Modesto, California, or St. Ann's Church in Hampton, New Jersey, or St. Patrick's Church in Kansas City, Kansas, or Washington, D.C.

Church means something universal and cosmic—and, at the same time, something local and intimate. It means something spiritual—and, at the same time, something concrete.

In the English New Testament we find Jesus using the word *church* in only two verses, and both times he is referring not to a building, but to the assembly of believers (see Matthew 16:18 and 18:17). Though in the first instance he speaks of construction and foundations, he is speaking metaphorically about the structure of authority that believers should one day observe. He said to the Apostle Simon: "And I tell you, you are Peter, and on this rock I will build my Church, and the gates of Hades shall not prevail against it" (Matthew 16:18).

In the later books of the New Testament—the Acts, the epistles, and Revelation—the word *church* is used mostly to describe local congregations: the church that meets in a certain city or a certain home. The Greek word used by the biblical authors is not *Kyriaké,* but *ekklesia,* from which we get our English word *ecclesiastical,* meaning "having to do with the Church."

In the Bible, the word *church* is never used to describe a building. That application came later, probably around

AD 300, and it was a natural association of the assembly of people with the place where the worshippers assembled. They're the Lord's people; they meet in the Lord's house. The Church meets at church.

In time, reflecting on the teaching of the Apostles, Christians would come to discern four "marks" of the true Church. These are recorded in the fourth-century Nicene Creed, which professes belief in a Church that is *one, holy, catholic,* and *apostolic.*

> *The Church is one.* Even in the Old Testament, God's people were seen as a community. The New Testament writers also emphasize that Christ's Church must be united. Only now the bond is much tighter. If Israel was a family of twelve tribes, the Church is described in terms of a single body! Saint Paul compares the

members of the Church to the limbs and organs of a body (see 1 Corinthians 12:12–27). Just as an arm can't stay alive apart from a torso, an individual can't be a Christian apart from the Church. For the Church is Christ's Body (Ephesians 1:22–23), and he is the head. Jesus himself identified himself with the Church when he asked Saul, the great persecutor of Christians, "Why do you persecute me?" Saul, after he converted to Christianity (and known as Saint Paul), insisted that "There is one body" (Ephesians 4:4; Colossians 3:15), not many bodies.

The Church is holy. Saint Paul also taught that Christians share the holiness of Jesus: "Christ loved the Church and gave himself up for her, that he might *sanctify* her"—that is, make her holy—"having cleansed her by the washing of water with the word, that he might present the Church to himself in splendor, without spot or wrinkle or any such thing, that she might be holy and without blemish" (Ephesians 5:25–27). Because its members have been washed in baptism, Saint Peter adds, the Church is now "a chosen race, a royal priesthood, a holy nation, God's own people" (1 Peter 2:9). Saint Paul uses the term "holy ones" (in Greek, *hagioi*) to describe the members of the Church (Colossians 1:2). In English we translate that word as "saints." Thus, another traditional term for the Church is the

"communion of saints," and this communion includes the members who live on earth and those
who are alive in heaven (whom Saint Paul calls
"saints in light," in Colossians 1:12).

The Church is catholic. Catholic is another word we
borrow from the Greek. It means "universal." It
means that Church membership is open to every
ethnic group, every race, every nation, and every
people upon the earth, and all are equals before
God. Jesus told the Apostles to "Go . . . and
make disciples of *all* nations" (Matthew 28:19)
and "you shall be my witnesses . . . to the end of
the earth" (Acts 1:8). As a result, many peoples
were represented when the Church was born on
the first Pentecost; Luke mentions more than a
dozen ethnicities in his account (Acts 2:9). Thus
the Christian church has been catholic since
the very beginning. *Catholic* means "universal,"
which means that the Church does not identify
itself with a political party or movement. The
Church does not belong to a particular earthly
empire or republic. The Church recognizes
Christ as King of Kings, and he reigns from
heaven. The earliest Christians gloried in the
name "catholic" because it points to something
revolutionary in the Christian religion. If God
is one, yet the Creator of many peoples, then
divine worship should unite all those whom he
has created.

The Church is apostolic. Christ never wrote a book. He did summon *Apostles*—that is, men who would be his emissaries to the world. He entrusted them with the sacraments, and they took the Good News of Jesus Christ to the nations. Most of the Apostles did not write books, but they did announce the coming of the Kingdom of God. They told the story of Jesus's life, death, Resurrection, and Ascension to glory. And they administered the sacraments. They offered the Mass (1 Corinthians 11: 23–24). They baptized (Acts 2:41). Deacons ordained men for ministry (Acts 6:6). They absolved sins in confession (James 5:16), and they anointed the sick (James 5:14–15). It was the Apostles who established the Church's authority, ritual life, and Scriptures. Their work continues today in the office of bishops, whose succession from the original twelve has been continuous and is verifiable (CCC 1555–1556).

The Church is at once heavenly and earthly. When we say the Church is "one," we mean not only that it unites people all over the world, but also that it unites the faithful on earth with the saints and angels in heaven. The shared worship of heaven and earth is a distinctive feature of the New Testament. The Letter to the Hebrews (12:22–24) describes the Church of the "first-born" children of God

worshipping on earth while mingling with angels. The saints look on as a "great cloud of witnesses" (Hebrews 12:1). The book of Revelation depicts Christian worship in similar terms: a "multitude" of human beings and angelic beings worshipping side by side (see Revelation 19:1). In both books the common worship is portrayed in terms of the Church's liturgy—with an altar and incense, chalices and manna, hymns and canticles, readings and petitions. It is a "festal" gathering, where one Church, made up of people from every time and place, gathers together in prayer.

It is the *heavenly* element that makes the Church "holy." We sing in a popular hymn to God: "Only thou art holy; there is none beside thee." And that's true. Holiness is a quality that belongs properly to God alone; and all Christians on earth recognize that they are sinners in need of forgiveness. Yet God has chosen to share his holiness with all his adopted children—in the Church, and through the Catholic sacraments, which are celebrated in Christian churches. So water flows from the church in baptism, with a "river of the water of life, bright as crystal, flowing from the throne of God and of the Lamb" (Revelation 22:1).

The Church's heavenly dimension also challenges us to expand our limited notions of the term *catholic*. Because the Church is universal, it must include those who have gone before us and those who will come after us. The communion of saints is vast. It contains multitudes.

Apostolic, too, refers not only to the labors of the twelve Apostles as they took the Gospel outward from Jerusalem. From the last book of the Bible we learn that, even in heaven, the Apostles serve as "foundation stones" of the City of God. Their vocation was not the task of a generation, completed at their death. It continues today. From heaven they continue to accompany the pilgrim Church on earth.

Whenever the Church on earth gathers for worship, it worships with the Church of heaven. In the penitential prayers at the beginning of Mass, the members of the congregation acknowledge this fact as they confess their sins in the presence of "all the angels and saints" as witnesses.

Catholic doctrine of the Church is made manifest not only in the prayers of the liturgy, but in every detail of construction and ornament in a church building. As the medieval monk Hugh of Saint Victor put it: "The material church, in which the people come together to praise God, signifies the Holy Catholic Church, which is built in the heavens of living stones."[1]

Here is another application of the sacramental principle. In every church, invisible realities shine through the visible ornaments. Something spiritual shines through all the material elements, inside and out. The ritual book for blessing a church offers a basic explanation of this symbolism: "The church is a visible building that stands as a special sign of the pilgrim Church on earth and reflects the Church dwelling in heaven."[2]

God created our bodily senses to lead us to spiritual truth. Thus, Catholic churches engage the human body as God created it. Eyes delight in seeing the play of light through stained glass. When Christians gather for worship, the church is full of the sound of music and sometimes the aroma of incense. Fingers touch stone and wood and dip into holy water. A church well built is a feast for the senses, a festival of praise for the God who fashioned the human body.

Grace builds on nature, heals it, and elevates it. This is one of the fundamental notions in Catholic theology, and it is also a key to understanding what one sees and hears and senses in a church.

A church is filled with *natural* pleasures; but in their context, *in church,* they conspire to lead Christians to a worship that is *supernatural.* The small details—incense and stones and water—are suggestive of the sights that Saint John described in the final chapters of the book of Revelation: the Marriage Supper of the Lamb, in the Heavenly Jerusalem. They are a foretaste and a promise.

The word *Church* (*ekklesia*) in the New Testament, like
the Hebrew word *qahal* in the Old Testament, corresponds
to an identifiable body of believers, an ordered society.
In ancient Israel it meant the assembly of God's Chosen
People—the members of the twelve tribes of Jacob. In the
New Testament, as we have seen, it means an assembly at
once in heaven and on earth—truly in heaven yet visible
on earth.

The Church is not just something invisible that God
will sort out at the end of time. It is something sacramental, already here, but not yet consummated.

From the time of the New Testament, the Catholic
Church has had a distinctive hierarchical form. Christ
called and appointed Apostles to serve all the members of
his Church. In the New Testament we see men holding
offices: bishop (see Titus 1:7), presbyter (sometimes trans-
lated as "elder"; see James 5:14), and deacon (see 1 Timothy 3:8). Over time, the word *presbyter* got shortened to
prester, and then *priest.*

The earliest Christian documents outside the Scriptures show that Christians everywhere observed these
three orders of clergy. The ancient writers note that this
was hardly a novelty: the New Testament orders corresponded to the Old Testament offices of high priest, priest,
and Levite.

From the beginning, Christians arranged their churches
to accommodate the hierarchical form of the Church. In
some places, each order of clergy—as well as many divi-

sions of laity—had assigned areas of seating. The sanctuary and altar were the province of the bishop and priests. The deacons fulfilled several roles, with corresponding stations: some proclaimed the Bible readings from the ambo; some preached sermons from the pulpit; some were assigned to guard the door in times of persecution. A fourth-century document speaks of reserving prominent seats for wayfarers, for the poor, and for consecrated virgins, adding that this was a tradition from the time of the Apostles. One of the oldest Christian writings, Saint Clement's *Letter to the Corinthians,* written in the first century, is an extended meditation on the respective and mutually beneficial roles of the clergy and laity.

The ancient churches, like the Church itself, had a certain form, and so were identifiable as Catholic. Saint Cyril of Jerusalem, preaching in the fourth century, warned his hearers not to be deceived by heretics in the neighborhood who were building structures in imitation of the Catholic model.

A church is built on faith to be perceived by faith. Michelangelo's devotion drove him to abandon all else to give his life to the construction of Saint Peter's. He did it, he said, for love of God.

In the Old Testament book of Exodus we meet a man named Bezalel, whom God calls to build the Tabernacle of Israel, and he is a man similarly "filled . . . with the Spirit of God, with ability and intelligence, with knowledge and all craftsmanship" (Exodus 31:3). His work is a divine vocation, not simply a construction job.

Though some churches become tourist attractions, their builders constructed them to be houses of prayer. They are buildings for worship, not simply pretty things to be browsed. When we contemplate their sacred art, we are receiving a message. Through the images, the artists are communicating the fruits of their own contemplation. When Leonardo da Vinci was in the midst of producing his *Last Supper,* he would spend *hours* without a brush in his hand, just staring at the unfinished wall, trying to place himself imaginatively in the Gospel scene with Christ and each of the Apostles. From such contemplation came art that is sacred and that inspires prayer still today.

The French architectural historian Jean Bony wrote of

the Gothic cathedrals in Paris and Chartres: "Their design transcribes . . . what is going on behind them, and expresses what was believed by the architects."[3]

The design expresses what the architects and artists believed—and what is going on, invisibly, inside. That statement could apply as easily to the designs that Michelangelo executed in Rome, and those of Justinian's architect Anthemius in Constantinople. They *believed*. They had faith in things unseen, and as a result, their churches express the spiritual in ways that are enduring; "for the things that are seen are transient, but the things that are unseen are eternal" (2 Corinthians 4:18).

What was begun in the Scriptures, and carried forward by saints such as Saint Clement of Rome, is today set out in clear principles in the Church's official documents. The *General Instruction of the Roman Missal* includes instructions for a church's interior design. "The People of God which is gathered for Mass is coherently and hierarchically ordered. . . . Hence the general arrangement of the sacred building must be such that in some way it conveys the image of the assembled congregation and allows the appropriate ordering of all the participants, as well as facilitating each in the proper carrying out of his function" (GIRM 294; see also 293).

Bishop, priest, deacon, lector, altar server, choir member, congregation—each has a distinct role to play, and the floor plan of a church should reflect those roles distinctly.

The *Catechism of the Catholic Church* gives a blueprint of a church based on the sacramental life of a Catholic congregation.

> The gathering of the People of God begins with Baptism; a church must have a place for the celebration of *Baptism* (baptistery) and for fostering remembrance of the baptismal promises (holy water font).
>
> The renewal of the baptismal life requires *penance*. A church, then, must lend itself to the expression of repentance and the reception of forgiveness, which requires an appropriate place to receive penitents.
>
> A church must also be a space that invites us to the recollection and silent prayer that extend and internalize the great prayer of the Eucharist. (1185)

Each church is a sign of the Church, alive with the power of Christ extended through his sacraments.

A traditional way to describe the Church is as *Mater et Magistra,* Mother and Teacher. A mother gives birth to her children and feeds them from her substance. At a parish's baptismal font, the Church gives new birth to children of God. At the altar, the Church feeds God's family with the Bread of Life, the Body of Christ. The Church is a mother, and every church is a mother

Like the Church, each church is a teacher, too. The Church teaches through the Scriptures, the writings of the saints, through homilies, through counsel in the confessional, and through the catechisms and official documents published by the pope and bishops. A parish church also teaches, though in a silent way, by the images depicted in its stained glass and artwork, through the symbols engraved on its altar—and, as we have seen, even through its very design and floor plan. There is a reason for everything. Every furnishing has something to teach us.

And the teaching is deeply doctrinal. There is one primary altar to symbolize the unity of the Church. There is one baptismal font because there is "one Lord, one faith, one baptism" (Ephesians 4:5). Windows are sometimes divided in three, to teach us that our one God is a Trinity of persons: Father, Son, and Holy Spirit.

The word *church* comes from *Kyriaké*—Greek for "belonging to the Lord." And everything about it, inside and outside, bears the marks of his ownership.

MYSTERIES OF THE CHURCH

A MYSTERY is a revealed truth that is above human understanding, but not contrary to reason. Mysteries are truths of Christian faith that the human mind could not figure out if God had not revealed them. Even a professor with a doctorate in mathematics could not demonstrate that God is a Trinity—three divine Persons, yet one God. Nor could researchers in a laboratory carry out experiments to prove that Jesus is really present in the Eucharist. Nor could X-rays or blood tests have shown that a carpenter from Nazareth was God Almighty, infinite and eternal. Human sciences stand lacking before the Incarnation of the Son of God.

We believe such mysteries not through induction or deduction, but because we trust the God who revealed them.

The Church is another mystery of Christian faith, and Jesus often spoke of it in mysterious terms. He said to his disciples: "To you has been given the secret [Greek: *mysterion*] of the kingdom of God, but for those outside everything is in parables" (Mark 4:11). Indeed, whenever Jesus spoke of the Church, he compared it with earthly things.

He called it a "kingdom," but he also compared it to a field sown with wheat and weeds, and to a fisherman's dragnet, and to a seed that becomes a mighty tree.

Jesus used many different images to describe his Church. The Apostles added to this treasury of imagery. Down the centuries, faithful Christians have further developed these depictions and woven them into the decoration and design of churches.

Theology is the name we give to the prayerful inquiry into the mysteries of God; and *ecclesiology* is the branch of theology that specifically explores the mystery of the Church. Since Jesus did not write a dictionary or reveal definitions, theologians in the field of ecclesiology meditate upon the images found in the Bible—images used to describe the Church in its various aspects, heavenly and earthly, seen and unseen, present and future.

Anyone who wants to understand the parts and symbols in a church should first take up a study of the biblical images favored by Jesus and his saints, especially the Apostles. These images will serve as lenses, enabling us to clarify and magnify the deeply mysterious things we encounter when contemplating a church.

In this chapter we'll consider just a few of those images, those most commonly employed by church architects and artists, and especially those that serve as *master ideas* in church design. Each of these images, all by itself, could be the subject of many books. In fact, some images have been. Here we can treat them only briefly, with the hope that readers may be led to deeper study in Scripture and ecclesiology.

The Body of Christ

Jesus spoke of a close and intimate bond uniting himself to believers. "I am the vine, you are the branches," he said (John 15:5). He went on to explain that each Christian would live *in* Christ and Christ would live *in* the believer. In the Gospels, Jesus speaks often of this communion, though he never uses the "body" metaphor explicitly to refer to the Church.

That happens for the first time in the Acts of the Apostles, when Jesus appears to the great persecutor of the Church, a Pharisee named Saul, and says to him: "Saul, Saul, why do you persecute me? . . . I am Jesus, whom you are persecuting" (Acts 9:4–5). Thus Jesus identified himself with the community that gathered in his name.

Saul became the great Apostle who took the Christian faith to the non-Jewish world, to the Gentiles. To that world he became known as Paul.

To Saint Paul the doctrine of the Church as Christ's body became supremely important. It is he who spelled it out in his letters to the churches he founded.

In his First Letter to the Corinthians, he explains that Christians are "one body" because they share the one bread (10:16–17), of which Christ had said, "This is my body" (11:24). He asks: "Do you not know that your bodies are members of Christ?" (1 Corinthians 6:15).

> For just as the body is one and has many members, and all the members of the body, though many, are one body, so it is with Christ. For by one Spirit we

were all baptized into one body—Jews or Greeks,
slaves or free—and all were made to drink of one
Spirit.

For the body does not consist of one member
but of many. (1 Corinthians 12:12–14)

As believers are the parts of the body of Christ, Saint Paul
goes on to explain, Christ is the head (1 Corinthians 11:3;
see also Ephesians 5:23–30 and Colossians 1:18).

This understanding leads Christians to a distinctive
way of life, a certain idea of moral behavior. The Apostle
asks: "Shall I therefore take the members of Christ and
make them members of a prostitute? Never!" (1 Corinthians 6:15).

Saint Paul's doctrine has also led Christians to a certain way of designing churches. From the time Christians
had the freedom to design churches from scratch, they designed them in the shape of a human body— more specifically, a body with its arms outstretched, a body hanging
on a cross. We will discuss this topic at length in the next
chapter.

The Temple

Judaism, in the time of Jesus, was a sacrificial religion,
centered on the offerings conducted according to the Law
of Moses. God permitted sacrifice in only one place: the
Jerusalem Temple. The Law required Jews living abroad to
make pilgrimage to the holy city three times a year—on

the feasts of Passover, Pentecost, and Tabernacles. Those who lived in the Diaspora, as far away as Rome or India, always built their synagogues to face in the direction of Jerusalem. If a Jewish traveler found himself far from a synagogue, he was still instructed to face the Temple when he prayed: "When a man rises to pray, if he is situated outside the land of Israel he should face toward Israel and direct his thoughts toward Jerusalem, the Temple, and the Holy of Holies."[1] In this way all the Chosen People could be united in divine worship as it took place daily in Jerusalem.

The Temple was an architectural marvel, built to reflect the glories of worship in heaven (see Wisdom 9:8). It was the privileged sanctuary of God's presence on earth, his dwelling place among his Chosen People. King Solomon built it at the urging of his father, David, and he spared no expense.

> The inner sanctuary was twenty cubits long, twenty cubits wide, and twenty cubits high; and he overlaid it with pure gold. He also made an altar of cedar. And Solomon overlaid the inside of the house with pure gold, and he drew chains of gold across, in front of the inner sanctuary. . . . Also the whole altar that belonged to the inner sanctuary he overlaid with gold. (1 Kings 6:19–22)

The Temple was built as "a house of prayer for all peoples" (Isaiah 56:7), not simply God's Chosen People. Foreigners were welcome to pray in the Court of the Gentiles. The people of Israel had access to inner precincts. Only the priests could enter the Holy Place; and only the high priest could enter the Holy of Holies—and only once a year on the Feast of Yom Kippur.

The Temple was built in the tenth century BC, destroyed by the Babylonians in 587 BC, rebuilt on a smaller scale in 516 BC—and then rebuilt on a grand scale by King Herod and his heirs in the first century AD, during Jesus's lifetime.

For a pious Jew, the Temple was the spiritual center of gravity on earth, dazzling in every way. Once, while visiting on pilgrimage, the disciples said to Jesus: "Look, Teacher, what wonderful stones and what wonderful buildings!" Jesus replied: "Do you see these great buildings? There will not be left here one stone upon another, that will not be thrown down" (Mark 13:1–2).

Jesus foresaw that the Temple would be utterly destroyed. In AD 70 the Romans left nothing in place, and all that remains today is the massive retaining wall on the hillside (known since then as the Wailing Wall).

Indeed, the Temple was decommissioned when Jesus breathed his last on the cross. Saint Luke tells us, "the curtain of the temple was torn in two" (Luke 23:45).

Jesus had predicted this turn of events. When he drove the moneychangers away, he said: "Destroy this temple, and in three days I will raise it up" (John 2:19). Then Saint John added: "He spoke of the temple of his body" (John 2:21).

Knowing what we know, it is clear to us why Jesus's body is a temple. He is the Word made flesh, God incarnate, so his body is the temple of God's presence in the world.

This brings us back to the notion of the Church as Christ's Body. Even while the Jerusalem Temple was still standing, Saint Paul made the obvious connection: If the Church is Jesus's body, it is also God's temple. "We are the temple of the living God," he wrote (2 Corinthians 6:16). "Do you not know that you are God's temple and that God's Spirit dwells in you? . . . God's temple is holy, and that temple you are" (1 Corinthians 3:16–17).

The members of the Church, Saint Paul explained, are "built upon the foundation of the apostles and prophets, Christ Jesus himself being the cornerstone, in whom the whole structure is joined together and grows into a holy temple in the Lord; in whom you also are built into it for a dwelling place of God in the Spirit" (Ephesians 2:20–22).

Christians, Saint Peter would add, are the "living stones" in a "spiritual house," all for the sake of "priesthood" and "sacrifice" (1 Peter 2:5). This is what Christians do when they gather for Mass in their churches.

Both the physical Temple and the spiritual temple it foreshadowed—the Church—have had a profound influence on Christians as they built their churches, and as they've interpreted the churches they have built.

The Tabernacle (Tent)

Before Israel had a fixed place of worship in the Temple, God made his dwelling in an elaborate tent (Latin:

tabernaculum), which God commanded Moses to build. The portable shrine, appropriate for a nomadic people, housed the relics of Israel's sojourn in the desert. In its inner sanctum was the Ark of the Covenant, containing the tablets of the Ten Commandments, the manna God had sent to feed the people, Aaron's rod, and the mercy seat. Before the Ark stood the seven-branched lampstand known as the Menorah. Though the Tabernacle was constructed of fabric and wood, it was decorated as lavishly and piously as the Temple of stone (see Exodus 35). The Temple copied the Tabernacle's floor plan and incorporated its contents. The Tabernacle would also influence the builders of Christian churches.

The Garden of Eden

At the beginning of creation, God made the garden intending to remain present there for humankind (Genesis 2:8). The earth was to be his sanctuary, with Adam tending and guarding it as a priest. But the first couple desecrated the sanctuary. God cleansed the garden by expelling them, placing cherubim to guard it from future profanation (Genesis 3:24). When Israel constructed the Tabernacle and then the Temple, God instructed them to decorate the holy places with images from nature. The first-century Jewish historian Josephus said that the decorations were "made in imitation and representation of the universe."[2] There were carved figures of gourds, palm trees, pomegranates, and open flowers; a bronze sea; the colors of sky and fire (1 Kings 6 and elsewhere). In both the Tabernacle and the Temple, images of the cherubim stood guard at the Holy of Holies (2 Chronicles 3:10). God's presence purifies and redeems fallen nature. The Lord reigns over the cosmos and brings about its restoration. Symbols from nature adorned the holy places of Israel and, later, the churches dedicated to Jesus Christ.

The Apocalypse

No book has exercised as profound an influence on Church decoration as the last book of the Bible, the book of Revelation. Though its imagery unscrolls in a way that defies simple narrative or description, it is vivid and memorable—and mostly related to ways God's people conducted their ritual worship. Thus we see an altar attended by vested priests, golden bowls of incense, chalices, a sacrificial Lamb of God, and so on. The saints and angels are gathered together in great numbers, as when "all Israel" gathered for worship in the assembly (Hebrew: qahal) of the Old Testament (see Exodus 35:1). In the New Testament, that assembly is the Church, in which heaven and earth are united in common worship. The Apocalypse provides motifs that never go out of style in Church art and design, though each age appropriates them in its own way. A prominent art historian observed: "The Gothic architect sought to represent the splendor of the city that, according to the Book of Revelation, was of 'pure gold,

like to clear glass.' But so did the Romanesque builder."[3]
And so should our contemporaries.

The Ship

In the New Testament, Saint Peter compares baptism to
Noah's ark. Through both, people are "saved through
water" (1 Peter 3:21; see also 2 Peter 2:5). The Church
is a refuge of safety and salvation on a sea of peril. Why?
Because Christ is present in this "ship." Thus the early
Christians also compared the Church to the "barque of
Peter," which Jesus rescued from the storm and the roiling
waves (Matthew 8:23–27).

A Christian of the second century put it eloquently:
"That little ship presented a figure of the Church, which is
disquieted 'in the sea,' that is, in the world, 'by the waves,'
that is, by persecutions and temptations. The Lord pa-
tiently sleeps, as it were, till roused by the prayers of the
saints, who have reached their limit. He checks the world
and restores tranquility to his own."[4]

Churches from earliest times have been designed to
suggest nautical themes. A fourth-century ritual book
instructs each bishop to see himself "as commander of a
great ship." The bishop should

> assign the deacons as mariners to prepare places
> for the congregation with all due care and de-
> cency, just as they would for passengers. And let

the building be long, with its head to the east, with its vestries on both sides at the east end, and so it will be like a ship. In the middle let the bishop's throne be placed, and on each side of him let the priests sit down; and let the deacons stand nearby . . . for they are like the mariners and managers of the ship.[5]

Kingdom

The most important message in the Gospel of Jesus Christ is the announcement that the Kingdom of God has arrived. It is a spiritual reality, and thus invisible (see Luke 17:20–21). Yet the Kingdom is known by certain visible manifestations (see Luke 7:20–22). *The Catechism of the Catholic Church* tells us: "The Church is the seed and beginning of this kingdom" (CCC 567). Because Jesus is King of Kings and the Church is the seed of his Kingdom, Christian churches have often been built to resemble royal courts and palaces. They are sometimes adorned by crowns, thrones, and other symbols of monarchy.

Mother

The people of Israel looked to Jerusalem as children look to their mother (see Isaiah 66:10–13). In Revelation 12 we see "a woman" laboring to give birth. She is the revealed to be the mother of the Messiah and "other offspring."

Scholars and saints have interpreted the figure variously to be Israel, the Church, and the Blessed Virgin Mary. It is likely that they are all correct, as biblical symbols often speak to many levels of meaning.

In early Christian literature, motherhood is probably the most popular metaphor for the Church's life and work.[6] Motherhood emerges often in ancient Christian art and inscriptions as well, again as a symbol of the Church's tender care for all believers. When the Blessed Virgin appears in frescoes, for example, she appears as the face of the Church, which bears Christ to the world.

The early Church Fathers often spoke of a church's baptismal font as the womb of the Church. At the baptistery at the Basilica of St. John Lateran, there is an inscription that proclaims this truth poetically:

> Here is born a people of noble race, destined for Heaven. . . . Mother Church conceives her offspring by the breath of God, and bears them virginally in this water.

THE SHAPE OF A CHURCH

A PARISH does not always have the luxury of shopping for the piece of land that's ideal for the site of a church. Sometimes they must make do with odd-shaped lots or the single spare sliver of an urban block. Christians worship where they can, and the Church has made use of all manner of properties to build churches in a wide variety of styles and shapes.

We are living, moreover, at the end of an unprecedented period of experimentation in church architecture. It's hard to think of a configuration that has not been tried in the last half-century.

So it's difficult to make generalizations about the geometry of worship. It is true, however, to say that a majority of churches built through the centuries were built according to a traditional pattern. They were built cruciform.

The traditional ground plan of a Christian church traces the form of a cross—or, more specifically, a crucified man. The long part of the cross is called the *nave,* and this is the place for the congregation. At the head of the cross is the *apse.* Between the nave and the apse are two "arms" extending out at right angles from the nave; these are called *transepts.*

It is, perhaps, stating the obvious to point out that churches are built this way to serve as images of the Church, which is the Body of Christ. In the case of a very large church, it can be almost impossible to discern the building's pattern at a glance. In the case of a city church, there may be no ground-level vantage point from which the cross shape is visible. It doesn't matter. The cruciform outline is visible from above, from "heaven," from where God the Father looks lovingly down upon the Son.

A church's main altar is usually placed in the apse, to represent Christ as the head of the body, according to Saint Paul's teaching. The altar is where the priest stands, in the person of Christ, to offer the Holy Sacrifice of the Mass, which is mystically united with Jesus's sacrifice on the cross at Calvary.

The Greek and Latin roots of the word *apse* are descriptive. The word suggests a curved form, an arch or a loop; and in many churches the apse is a semicircular extension of the building.

It is an ancient custom to place the apse at the eastern end of the church. The early Christians testified that the Apostles had instructed them to pray facing east,[1] just as the Jews of that time always prayed facing Jerusalem. Why did the Apostles face east? Perhaps because they expected Jesus to return from that direction. After all, he had told them: "For as the lightning comes from the east and shines as far as the west, so will be the coming of the Son of man" (Matthew 24:27). And the sign that heralded Jesus's first advent, in Bethlehem, was a "star in the East" (Matthew 2:1–2). At the dawn of creation, "the Lord God planted a garden in Eden, in the east" (Genesis 2:8).

Searching the prophets of the Old Testament, they found many oracles to confirm their belief. So says the Prophet Zechariah: "On that day his feet shall stand on the Mount of Olives which lies before Jerusalem on the east" (Zechariah 14:4). Speaking through the Prophet Malachi, the Lord compares his return to a sunrise—which, of course, takes place on the eastern horizon: "But for you who fear my name the sun of righteousness shall rise, with healing in its wings" (Malachi 4:2). The most powerful testimony, however, comes from the Prophet Ezekiel: "And behold, the glory of the God of Israel came from the east. . . . As the glory of the Lord entered the temple by the gate facing east, the Spirit lifted me up, and brought me into the inner court; and behold, the glory of the Lord filled the temple" (Ezekiel 43:2, 4–5).

So firm was this Christian custom that graves in churchyard cemeteries were also placed facing eastward, so that the dead could rise immediately to greet the Lord.

The apse contains the church's "holy place," its *sanctuary*, and so a church traces the layout of the Jerusalem Temple.

In order to emphasize the special quality of the sanctuary, the Church requires that it "should be appropriately marked off from the body of the church either by its
being somewhat elevated or by a particular structure and
ornamentation" (GIRM 295). This rule applies whether
a church is like a cross or round, square, or octagonal.
The altar stands in a place that is separate from the
congregation.

In the Eastern Church, the sanctuary is hidden from
view behind a screen of sacred images, called the *iconosta-
sis*. Western churches, too, kept *rood screens* or *chancel screens*
in front of their sanctuaries until the sixteenth century.
Some of these remain in place in older cathedrals.

As in the Jerusalem Temple, so in the churches: There
was a clear division between the courts and the holy place,
and access to the latter was restricted to those involved in
the church's ministries.

Writing in the fourth century, the historian Eusebius
drew out the comparison between the old Temple and the
new form of temple. He referred to a new church in Tyre
as "this temple built of you yourselves, a living temple of
a living God, the greatest truly majestic sanctuary, I say,
whose innermost shrines are hidden from the mass of men
and are in truth a Holy Place and a Holy of Holies." In the
Holy of Holies, only the High Priest, Jesus, is permitted
to enter.[2]

In Eusebius's day, the sanctuary was reserved for the
clergy, the nave for the baptized laity, and the vestibule for
non-Christians and for Christians who had sinned griev-
ously and were living penitentially to make up for their

sins. Thus, the structure of the Christian temple corresponded to that of the Jerusalem Temple, which foreshadowed it.

The distinctions remain the same today as in the first century, when Saint Clement wrote: "Unto the high priest his proper services have been assigned, and to the priests their proper office is appointed, and upon the Levites their proper ministrations are laid. The layman is bound by the layman's ordinances. . . . Let each of you, brethren, in his own order give thanks unto God, maintaining a good conscience and not transgressing the appointed rule of his service, but acting with all seemliness."[3]

This rankles modern sensibilities, perhaps. This age tends to prize egalitarianism above everything. But a church's interior stands as a sign for worshippers: so that the faithful on earth always remember the sacred order of creation and redemption. We are not God, and we are not the canonized saints of heaven just yet.

Saint Maximus the Confessor observed in the seventh century: "God's holy church in itself is a symbol of the sensible world, since it keeps the divine sanctuary as heaven and the beauty of the nave as earth." Referring back to a church's cruciform shape, he also said: "The holy church is like a man because for the soul it has the sanctuary, for mind it has the divine altar, and for body it has the nave."[4]

The floor plan is there for a reason: to highlight the temple where God dwells, to manifest the body that makes all Christians one Body, to point the way to God's eternal sanctuary in heaven.

CHURCHES AND
OTHER WORSHIP SPACES

THE WORD *church* is usually applied to the main building
dedicated to divine worship in a parish or diocese. But
other terms crop up when we consider Catholic worship.
Each of these applies to a different sort of structure, with
its own special purpose.

Cathedral is the name given to the chief church of a diocese.
A cathedral is the local bishop's official church, where he
presides, teaches, and leads worship for the whole Christian
community. Cathedrals take their name from the Greek
word for chair, *kathedra*. In the ancient world, philosophers
and professors taught their disciples while seated in such a
chair. The chair became a symbol of their authority.

In the Church, the *cathedra* refers to the bishop's chair located in the sanctuary of the cathedral church. In this context, the chair is the symbol of the bishop's role as chief shepherd of the local church and teacher of the faith. It is a symbol, too, of the Church's apostolic character, since the bishop holds his office in direct succession from the Apostles.

Some of the world's most famous churches are cathedrals, such as Notre Dame in Paris, St. Patrick's in New York, and the Duomo in Florence. The cathedral church

of Rome is not St. Peter's Basilica, as many people sur-
mise, but the Basilica of St. John Lateran.

Basilica refers to a certain type of building associated with
official functions of kings in the ancient world. The Greek
word *basileius* means "house of the king." These buildings were oblong, usually rectangular, with an apse at one
end. Basilicas were among the first secular buildings to be
adapted for sacred use when Christianity was legalized in the
fourth century. Their structure, easily divided into nave and
sanctuary, was well suited for the celebration of the Mass.
Among the major churches of Rome are several ancient basilicas: St. John Lateran, St. Peter's, St. Mary Major, St. Paul
Outside the Walls, and St. Lawrence Outside the Walls.

In recent years, the Church has used the term *basilica*
as an honorific title for certain churches of historical or
other significance, regardless of whether they are built in
the old Roman style. These are called *minor basilicas,* a title
that can be bestowed only by the pope. Their privilege is
marked by certain decorations, including the papal coat of
arms, displayed at the church entrance or in the sanctuary,
and the *ombrellino,* a "little umbrella" in the papal colors, of
the sort that was used to shade the pope when he traveled.

A *shrine* is a place approved by the local bishop as a
pilgrimage destination. Shrines are intended to foster piety,
expressed especially in the celebration of the Mass and sacramental confession. Through history, shrines have often
been the tombs or repositories of the relics of the saints.

Some shrines are designated *national shrines* by their country's conference of bishops. A beautiful example is the Basilica of the National Shrine of the Immaculate Conception—sometimes simply called the National Shrine—in Washington, D.C. It is a church specially devoted to the Blessed Virgin, under the title of the Immaculate Conception, for it is under that title that she is patroness of the United States. There are other national shrines in the United States, some of them dedicated to the memory of saints, such as the National Shrine of St. Jude in Chicago and the National Shrine of the Little Flower (Saint Thérèse) in Royal Oak, Michigan.

A *chapel* is a room, area, or building that can be used for prayer or for Holy Mass. A chapel may be freestanding, or it may be an area within a larger church, or a room within a school, hospital, or convent.

The word *chapel* comes from the Latin word for cape. The tent that was used to enshrine the cape of Saint Martin of Tours was known as the *cappella*. The name stuck when the relic moved to better quarters, and the term soon came to encompass any such area given to prayers and devotions.

An *oratory* is a chapel designated by the bishop for use by a specific community that is not a parish. The word means simply "place of prayer."

A *martyrium* is a church built to house the remains of one or more martyrs—or built at the site where the martyr or martyrs died for the faith. These structures were especially popular during the centuries of Roman imperial persecution and immediately afterward. Some martyria are small, simple shrines. Others, such as St. Peter's Basilica, are massive in size. Many martyria became popular as pilgrim destinations.

A *crypt* is a subterranean chamber beneath a church's main floor. In some churches, crypt chapels are used as burial places. When they are regularly used for Mass, some of these chapels are called *crypt churches*.

A *baptistery* (or *baptistry*) is a building, room, or area used for administering the sacrament of baptism. Baptisteries are usually located inside or adjacent to a parish church. Some of the baptisteries from ancient times are very large, freestanding structures that could accommodate the great number of conversions that the Church experienced in the fourth century. Many of these early baptisteries were eight-sided (octagonal), representing a new beginning, the eighth day of creation. A first-century document praises the Lord's ability to surpass even the glorious rest of the Sabbath, and to "usher in the Eighth Day, the beginning of a new world."[1]

THE SANCTUARY

A SANCTUARY is, literally, a holy place. It is a place reserved for the holy and protected from defilement. We
sometimes apply the term, metaphorically, to places where
animals can be free from threats by anything that is in-
compatible with the continuation of their lives—things
such as predators and sudden climate change.

God needs no such protection. But in biblical religion
a sanctuary is a place where the divine nature can dwell
free from profanation by sin. The Garden of Eden was
intended to be such a place. God created Adam to be a
priest; having dominion over the earth, he was to make
everything in creation a pure offering to God. He failed in
this task, so the sanctuary had to be purified of the taint of
sin. Adam and Eve were expelled, and their offspring—all
of humanity—could not enter into the rest and fulfillment
for which God had created them.

The Bible tells us that Israel's Tabernacle and Temple were to serve as "a copy and shadow of the heavenly sanctuary" (Hebrews 8:5). They were preserves of holiness in the world, tended by priests, who may have done their best but were still no less sinful than Adam had been.

Jesus Christ entered history as the Second Adam, to succeed where the first Adam had failed. Through his priesthood, he rendered the Jerusalem Temple obsolete (see Hebrews 9:8). By his Ascension into heaven, he "entered, not into a sanctuary made with hands, a copy of the true one, but into heaven itself, now to appear in the presence of God on our behalf" (Hebrews 9:24).

What happened in the Temple was a foreshadowing of Jesus's definitive saving action. The priests of the tribe of Levi could enter Jerusalem and "ascend the hill of the Lord . . . and . . . stand in his holy place" (Psalm 24:3). They could sing a "Song of Ascent." But all that was simply a prefigurement of the sinless Priest, Jesus, and his Ascension to heaven's glory.

The extension of that moment, for all time, occurs in the Holy Mass, which takes place in the sanctuary of the Church. The Catholic priest, who is specially conformed to Christ by the sacrament of holy orders, serves as an image of Christ when he processes to the altar. When he enters the sanctuary, he enters the place where God will come to dwell upon the altar. The priest enters heaven on earth, because heaven is the presence of God, and God is really present in the Eucharist.

Animal sacrifice was the hallmark of the rituals associated with the old sanctuary. The priests of Israel sacrificed sheep, goats, oxen, and other livestock that were ritually "clean" and thus eligible for an offering. The blood of those animals could not truly take away sin, but conferred a symbolic cleansing. The Blood of Christ, however, accomplishes what it signifies—perfect God and perfect Man—and so "we have confidence to enter the sanctuary by the blood of Jesus" (Hebrews 10:19).

When the Church offers the Body and Blood of Christ in the Eucharist, the offering takes place in the sanctuary of a church. The *General Instruction of the Roman Missal* explains: "The sanctuary is the place where the altar stands, the Word of God is proclaimed, and the Priest, the Deacon, and the other ministers exercise their functions" (GIRM 295).

The sanctuary's special dignity is reflected in its decoration. In some churches there are images of angels, as in the Holy Place of the Jerusalem Temple—and the entryway to the Garden of Eden. There are candles and vessels made of precious metal: gold and silver. Sometimes the walls or ceiling will be decorated with stars or with the image of a multitude of the saints of heaven.

In the ancient churches of the West—and still in the churches of the Eastern rites—the sanctuary is closed off from view by the congregation with a screen. Eusebius described one of these churches, newly built in the early fourth century. In the sanctuary were "lofty thrones in honor of those who preside . . . and finally placed in the middle the holy of holies, the altar, and, that it might be inaccessible to the multitude, enclosed . . . with wooden lattice-work, accurately wrought with artistic carving, presenting a wonderful sight to the beholders."[1]

The thrones and artwork are not for the honor of the clergy who preside there, nor simply for the delight of the onlookers. They are meant to inspire awe. The biblical patriarch Jacob woke from a dream of a stairway reaching up to heaven, and "he was afraid, and said, 'How awesome is this place! This is none other than the house of God, and this is the gate of heaven' " (Genesis 28:17). The Catholic Church uses those lines whenever a bishop blesses a new sanctuary. For, if Jacob stood awestruck from a mere *dream* of that stairway, Catholics stand at that gate, and should stand in awe, whenever they go to Mass, wherever they go to Mass. The decorations in a sanctuary reflect a glory unseen by the eyes of the body, but known to the eyes of faith. Christ has taken our humanity into heaven; and he brings heaven to earth, as a foretaste, in every Mass celebrated in his Church.

THE NAVE

WHEN THE ancient Greeks and Romans built their temples, they didn't need to trouble themselves by providing a place for a congregation. Pagan temples, by and large, had

no congregations. A god or goddess might have adherents, but these people fulfilled their duties mostly by paying for the sacrifices that were the business of the temple. Greco-Roman religion was not *personal* in the way Christianity and Judaism are, and it was only incidentally and occasionally communal.

Christianity, on the contrary, is intensely personal and communal, and a church's nave signifies those distinctive qualities.

The nave is a church's central open space, usually extending from the sanctuary to the front entryway of the church. It is the part of the building reserved for worshippers, and this makes it supremely important in the configuration of a church.

Blessed John Henry Newman once encountered a priest who spoke contemptuously of the lay members of the Church. "The laity," he said, "who are they?" Newman replied that "the Church would look foolish without them."

The Church would indeed look foolish without the laity, as a church would look foolish without worshippers. For it would look nothing like a Christian community.

The documents of the Church give ample attention to the requirements of the nave, with clear instructions for its design:

> Places for the faithful should be arranged with appropriate care so that they are able to participate in the sacred celebrations, duly following them with their eyes and their attention. It is desirable that

benches or seating usually should be provided for their use. However, the custom of reserving seats for private persons is to be reprobated. Moreover, benches or seating should be so arranged, especially in newly built churches, that the faithful can easily take up the bodily postures required for the different parts of the celebration and can have easy access for the reception of Holy Communion.

Care should be taken to ensure that the faithful be able not only to see the Priest, the Deacon, and the readers but also, with the aid of modern technical means, to hear them without difficulty. (GIRM 311)

Since most churches were built in the shape of a cruciform man, the nave signifies his body. The laity are not simply members of the Church, but members of Christ. There is a saying often attributed to St. Teresa of Avila. She may or may not have said it, but it is nonetheless true. "Christ has no body now on earth but yours, no hands but yours, no feet but yours. Yours are the eyes through which Christ's compassion is to look out to the earth. Yours are the feet by which he is to go about doing good, and yours are the hands by which he is to bless us now." It is the laity who bring Christ to the world.

A medieval commentator, Bishop William Durand, said that a church's nave offers a vision of the Church as a house of "living stones," as Saint Peter said it would be. "The faithful," said Bishop Durand, "are the stones in the structure of this wall which shall continually be built up until the world's end. And one stone is added to another. . . . Those stones that are larger, and polished or squared, are . . . those of holier life, who by their merits and prayers uphold weaker brethren in Holy Church."[1]

One of the ancient Fathers looked at his church and described it in terms of the philosophy of Aristotle. He said that the nave is the sanctuary in potency, and the sanctuary is the nave in act.[2] The nave represents earth striving toward divine life in heaven. God gives human beings the grace, and therefore the ability, to do this.

All of the faithful, clergy and laity alike, share in the one priesthood of Jesus Christ. By baptism, all are configured to Christ as members of his Body. But those in ministerial priesthood are configured to Christ as head of the Church, his Body. Thus, they carry out different responsibilities in the Church. Laypeople work in the world and offer their work, along with their family life and leisure time, to God whenever they attend Mass. In doing so, they consecrate the world itself to God.[3]

The origins of the word *nave* are uncertain. There are two strong possibilities, both of which evoke profound Christian meaning. Some say it comes from the Latin word *navis,* meaning "ship." This word is descriptive, since the nave is oblong, like a ship. It also evokes a wealth of biblical images, as we have already seen in another chapter, "Mysteries of the Church": Noah's ark and Peter's boat.

Others, however, say that the word *nave* comes from the Greek *naos,* meaning "temple." If so, it is a splendid irony. For it is Christ's Church that has rendered the old pagan temples obsolete. And the Catholic Church invites the whole world to God's house to share the heavenly banquet and to become Christ's Body on earth and his temple.

THE ALTAR

A CATHOLIC church is built for the sake of the altar. No other element, inside or outside the building, is so carefully regulated by canon law, pondered by theologians, revered by saints—and influential in church design and decoration.

In other places of worship, used by members of other religions, the most important item may be the pulpit or the congregational seating, and the layout of the church will serve that priority. But in a Catholic church everyone and everything is there in order to serve the altar.

It's difficult to exaggerate the altar's importance. The twentieth-century philosopher Josef Pieper, known for his subtle and sober prose, described a church building as "nothing other . . . than the structure which shelters and surrounds the altar." In fact, he added, the altar is "more important than the church building."

Pieper emphasized that the altar is not a mere piece of furniture: "On the one hand it is a table for a ritual meal, and on the other hand, it is at the same time a rock on which a sacrifice is performed."[1]

The religion of the Bible is a sacrificial religion, and sacrifices require *priests* to perform them and *altars* on which they can be performed. This fact is abundantly clear in the Old Testament. The Patriarch Abraham is described as a friend of God, but he does not express his love in an abundance of words. As the *Catechism* explains: "Abraham's prayer is expressed first by deeds: a man of silence, he constructs an altar to the Lord at each stage of his journey. Only later does Abraham's first prayer in words appear" (CCC 2570).

From the story of Cain and Abel through the oracles of Malachi, the story of the Old Testament is the story of the sacrificial offerings of God's Chosen People. Nor does this story end with the Old Testament. The New Testament Letter to the Hebrews is a summary retelling of the story, with its extension in the New Testament. In Hebrews we encounter Jesus as the new High Priest, entering the sanctuary of heaven and offering his once-for-all sacrifice of the cross. At the Last Supper he made the offering of his Body and Blood and established it as his perpetual memorial. He spoke of what he was doing using terms that had clear sacrificial meaning for first-century Jews. He made the offering, moreover, at a Passover meal, which was itself a ritual sharing in the Temple's sacrifice.

He established his sacrifice in clear continuity with all that had gone before, and the Letter to the Hebrews makes this clear, tracing Jesus's sacrificial lineage back to Melchizedek and Abel, both characters from the book of Genesis. The author of the Letter to the Hebrews writes: "We have an altar from which those who serve the tent [that is, the Tabernacle] have no right to eat" (Hebrews 13:10).

Christians do indeed have an altar, and it is the centerpiece and focal point of their churches. Christians, too, celebrate a Passover. Our rites have a "paschal" character. But ours is the new Passover of Jesus Christ, who has crossed the great divide between earth and heaven, overcoming the sin and death that separated humanity from happiness and fulfillment in God. This is the Christian Passover, celebrated in the house of God, in communion with the altar of heaven (see Revelation 8:3–5). Saint Paul said: "Christ, our Paschal Lamb, has been sacrificed" (1 Corinthians 5:7), and in the very next verse he explained that we celebrate the Lord's new festival with the "unleavened bread" that is the Lord's Body.

The altar is the reason Christians build churches. In

gathering before the altar, they fulfill the will of Christ for the salvation of humanity. It has been that way from the beginning. One of the early Fathers, Saint John Chrysostom, preached: "This altar is an object of wonder: by nature it is stone, but it is made holy when it receives the Body of Christ."[2] Chrysostom made clear that the Mass is not the work of human beings. No creature can compel God or draw down holiness. The sacrifice of the Christian altar is a divine action. Christ is both priest and victim, though for the sake of his Church he shares his priesthood with earthly ministers. "We indeed see a man," said Chrysostom, "but it is God who acts through him. *Nothing human takes place at this holy altar* [emphasis ours]."[3]

Long before Chrysostom, Saint Irenaeus of Lyons, in the second century, explained the how and why of this interchange between heaven and earth. He described a communion between the Church's altar and the altar of heaven.

Now we make offering to him, not as though he needed it, but giving thanks for his gift, and thus sanctifying what has been created. For even though God does not need our possessions, we do need to offer something to God. . . . God lacks nothing, but takes our good works to himself for this purpose: so that he may grant us a recompense of his own good things. . . . He does not need these [services], yet he desires that we should render them for our own benefit. . . . So did the Word give to the people that very precept for the making of oblations, although he had no need for them,

that they might learn to serve God. Thus is it his
will that we, too, should offer a gift at the altar,
frequently and without stint. The altar, then, is in
heaven; for toward that place our prayers and oblations are directed. The Temple likewise [is there],
as John says in Revelation—"And the Temple of
God was opened" (Revelation 11:19)—the Tabernacle also—"For, behold," he says, "the Tabernacle of God, in which he will dwell with men"
(Revelation 21:3).[4]

The theology of the altar was deeply developed very
early in the life of the Church. The fourth-century historian Eusebius set Christian history in continuity with the
history of Israel. He showed the Church's altar to be the
heavenly earthly fulfillment of Temple and Tabernacle:

But the great and august and unique altar, what
else could this be than the pure holy of holies
of the soul of the common priest of all? Standing at the right of it, Jesus himself, the great High
Priest of the universe, the Only Begotten of God,
receives with bright eye and extended hand the
sweet incense from all, and the bloodless and im-
material sacrifices offered in their prayers, and
bears them to the heavenly Father and God of the
universe. And he himself first worships him, and
alone gives to the Father the reverence which is his
due, beseeching him also to continue always kind
and propitious to us all.[5]

The Church's faith and the Church's practice have remained unchanged since the time of the Apostles. Christian altars, however, have undergone some changes through the years.

In the beginning, as we have said, Christians worshipped where they could—in homes and shops and even outdoors. Archaeology and textual studies seem to indicate that the earliest altars were made of wood. They were likely the tables already standing in the dining rooms and workrooms where Christians secretly met.

After Constantine's legalization of Christianity, altars made of stone gradually became the norm, at least for churches in the Roman world.

Church law jealously preserves the altar's special place in Christian life. Canon law insists that when Mass is offered in a church, it "must be carried out on a dedicated or blessed altar" (CIC 932 §2); outside a sacred place a suitable table can be used for Mass, just as in the olden days.

Canon law prescribes that each church should have one primary "fixed" altar, to "signify the one Christ and the one Eucharist of the Church" (GIRM 303). An altar is fixed if "it adheres to the floor and thus cannot be moved" (CIC 1235 §1). The *mensa,* or table portion of the altar, should be made of stone, according to the traditional practice of the Church. "Nevertheless," the law allows, "another worthy and solid material can also be used in the judgment of the conference of bishops. The supports or base, however, can be made of any material" (CIC 1236 §1). In the United States, wood is allowed, as long as it "is dignified, solid, and well-crafted" and "the altar is structurally immobile" (GIRM 301). On the surface of the mensa, five crosses are carved (or otherwise represented), one at each corner and one in the center, to represent the five wounds of Christ.

When a bishop dedicates a church, he spends a large portion of the rite anointing and blessing the altar. This is, indeed, the most important part of the church, so it is the most important part of the ritual. Once an altar has been blessed, it is reserved exclusively for divine worship and nothing else can transpire there. It may not be used for a meal or a meeting, for example, no matter how solemn or important.

The Church's regulations also protect the clarity of the altar's symbolism, restricting its decoration to keep it simple: "Moderation should be observed in the decoration of the altar" (GIRM 305). Only the vessels, fabrics, and books required for the celebration of the Mass may be placed on the altar table (GIRM 306).

Candlesticks are placed either on the altar or around it. They are an important part of the altar's symbolism, since Jesus Christ revealed himself to be "the light of the world" (John 8:12 and 9:5).

The altar draws together all the mysteries of Christ's life in a single saving moment. The early Christians saw the altar as a symbol both of his cross and of the tomb from which he rose (see CCC 1182). They saw it as the site of a preview and foretaste of heavenly glory, but also as a re-membrance of the long-ago glories of the Holy of Holies.

The Church experiences all of this in a single point in time, in the Mass, at this singular place in the sanctuary.

PEWS AND KNEELERS

JUST AS the things in the sanctuary must accommodate the duties of the clergy, so the things in the nave must suit the duties of the laity. The priest has his rules to follow in the course of the Mass, and laypeople have theirs. The church is built with this in mind. The role of the congregation has implications for church design and decoration.

Catholic worship is distinctive in terms of the postures and gestures prescribed for the congregation. Converts often say they need time to adjust to the Sunday round of standing, sitting, kneeling, and standing again. It is a form of communication—body language—that expresses the range of an individual's relations with God. To stand is to show respect, as one would if a great dignitary walked into the room. To kneel is to express extreme adoration and supplication; it is an unusual posture in Western culture, reserved almost solely for divine worship. To sit is to

render oneself defenseless, open, receptive; a congregation sits for the proclamation of the Scriptures (other than the Gospel) and for the homily.

Catholic worship involves not just the soul and the voice, but the whole body and all the senses. Worshipping with the body is a deeply biblical notion, and it makes for effective prayer: When Abram prostrated himself, God spoke to him (see Genesis 17:3).

The ancient churches were not exactly built for comfort. During the centuries of persecution, Christians had to hide in order to worship, so congregations often had to squeeze into small inner chambers in family homes. Even later when the faith was legal, the great basilicas placed a premium on awe, not ease. Clergy and laity alike were expected to stand through most, if not all, of the Mass. A church might have a few benches to accommodate worshippers who were ill or elderly, but these were an exception. The space for the congregation was mostly wide open. Not until the late Middle Ages did a growing number of churches begin to provide backless benches or chairs; kneelers are a much more recent innovation. For most of history, Christians knelt on the bare floors of their churches, or on whatever cushion they could fashion from a rolled-up overcoat.

Times have certainly changed. Today the *General Instruction of the Roman Missal* prescribes a "suitable arrangement of a church" that is "conducive to their [the faithful's] appropriate comfort." People should expect a church to be as comfortable as other "places where people habitually gather" (GIRM 293). So today congregations pray using the latest innovations: pews in which to sit and kneelers on which to rest the knees.

The U.S. Catholic bishops give more specific and practical directions. A pew or chair should be situated so that members of the congregation can "see the ministers at the altar, the ambo, and the chair."[1] Nor should a church skimp on these furnishings for worshippers: "Since the liturgy requires various postures and movements, the space and furniture for the congregation should accommodate them well. Styles of benches, pews, or chairs can be found that comfortably accommodate the human form. Kneelers or kneeling cushions should also be provided so that the whole congregation can easily kneel when the liturgy calls for it."[2]

A church's interior should reflect the Church's theology of the laity. Worshippers are not spectators at the liturgy. They are "a chosen race, a royal priesthood, a holy nation, God's own people" (1 Peter 2:9). Their participation should be "full, conscious, and active."[3] Thus, said the U.S. bishops, "Parishes will want to choose a seating arrangement that calls the congregation to active participation and that avoids any semblance of a theater or an arena."[4]

The laity's common priesthood extends to *all* the baptized, so a church should be accessible to young and old, people who are sick and people with disabilities. With baptism comes a sweet obligation to attend Mass on Sundays and holy days. A church's construction can make it possible or impossible, easy or difficult, for people to fulfill that duty. Jesus said: "When you give a feast, invite the poor, the maimed, the lame, the blind" (Luke 14:13). The bishops have asked parishes to make accessibility a priority when they build or renovate churches. This instruction merely echoes the Apostle's call for Christians to "make straight paths for your feet, so that what is lame may not be put out of joint but rather be healed" (Hebrews 12:13).

THE CRUCIFIX

"O FOOLISH Galatians! Who has bewitched you, before whose eyes Jesus Christ was publicly portrayed as crucified?" (Galatians 3:1).

As Saint Paul took the Gospel out to the wide world, he had to acknowledge a horrifying and scandalous truth: Jesus, the God-man, had undergone the most shameful and humiliating public torture—a death reserved for slaves, traitors, and other lowlifes. He had been crucified. The Jewish historian Josephus called crucifixion "the most wretched of deaths."[1] It was designed to cause the most pain in the most parts of the body over the longest period of time. It was designed for humiliation as well. The victim was stripped and exposed naked to a mob that mocked him and pelted him with rocks or trash.

Yet Paul dared to "glory" in the cross of Jesus Christ (Galatians 6:14), and he placed Jesus's Crucifixion at the

heart of his preaching: "The cross is folly to those who are perishing, but to us who are being saved it is the power of God" (see 1 Corinthians 1:18–25).

It is foolishness. It is a stumbling block. Nevertheless it is God's power, made perfect in utter weakness, utter shame, and the utmost physical pain. The Crucifixion is at the center of the Gospel, and so it is placed at the center of gravity, the center of action, in every Catholic church.

Jesus Christ must be, as Saint Paul said, "publicly portrayed as crucified." The *General Instruction of the Roman Missal* directs that "either on the altar or near it, there is to be a cross, with the figure of Christ crucified upon it, a cross clearly visible to the assembled people" (GIRM 308). The directive goes on to recommend "that such a cross should remain near the altar even outside of liturgical celebrations, so as to call to mind for the faithful the saving Passion of the Lord."

The U.S. Catholic bishops, in their guidelines for art, architecture, and worship, speak of the practical spiritual benefit of placing a crucifix at the visible center of a Catholic church: "The cross with the image of Christ crucified is a reminder of Christ's paschal mystery. It draws us into the mystery of suffering and makes tangible our belief that our suffering when united with the passion and death of Christ leads to redemption."[2]

To unbelievers, the crucifix is an image of folly and shame, but believers are foolish only when they forget what the Crucifixion means. The crucifix reminds Catholics of what is taking place on that altar, what the Church is doing, as Jesus commanded it to do, "in remembrance." The Mass makes present the one sacrifice of Christ on the cross.

The Holy Sacrifice of the Mass is the sacrifice of the cross, and a church's crucifix is the public reminder of that. As Saint Paul put it: "Christ loved us and gave himself up for us, a fragrant offering and sacrifice to God" (Ephesians 5:2).

Yet he was not a priest remote from the people, shut off by himself in the holy place. He came down to share in our suffering, even to the point of death on the cross.

The art historian Margaret Visser begins her book *The Geometry of Love* with a tale about a Japanese tourist whose first introduction to Christianity occurred when he engaged a guide to walk him through a Spanish church.

> The guide told him, in English, the dates of various ous parts of the building and then proceeded to

dilate upon the superb stone vaulting. The tourist did not even raise his head to look at this. He stared aghast—as well he might—at a horrific, life-sized painted carving of a bleeding man nailed to two pieces of wood. When the guide had stopped talking, the man gestured wordlessly towards the statue. The guide nodded, smiled, and told him in which century it had been carved.[3]

Such was the horror of the ancient world, too, when confronted with the scandal of a tortured god. One of the earliest-known depictions of the Crucifixion is in *anti*-Christian graffiti found in an excavation in Rome. Pagans wanted to remind believers of the *shame* at the center of their religion.

Christians, for their part, would not have needed a reminder. Criminals were crucified often at the outskirts of town. Crucifixion was a familiar sight in the Greco-Roman world, so the Gospel writers did not need to dwell on it or describe it in detail. "And they crucified him" is all Saint Mark says at the climax of his story (15:24).

But congregations in the first century did need a reminder, as Saint Paul pointed out to the "foolish Galatians." And people in the twenty-first century need to be reminded as well.

Christ the High Priest has only one sacrifice to offer, and it is his body. He made that offering at the Last Supper when he said, "This is my body. . . . This is the chalice of my blood." He consummated that offering on the cross, when his blood was poured out and he gave forth his Spirit. Then, when he rose from the dead and ascended into glory, he traced the path of the temple priest who entered the Holy of Holies in the Jerusalem Temple.

In heaven, Jesus made—and continues to make—his offering to God the Father. His offering is eternal, complete, and perfect. On earth, the very sign of that self-giving is the crucifix that stands by the altar.

Jesus's sacrifice is singular and perfect—on the cross, in heaven, and on the altar. From the altar, Jesus shares his life with the Church by means of the Mass. At the altar he gives his flesh for the life of the world, and that flesh is the "living bread which came down from heaven" (John 6:51).

The earliest house churches had no crucifixes and few crosses, though Christians would sometimes weave "crypto-crosses" into their church designs. With the legalization of Christianity came the abolition of crucifixion. Criminals were no longer tortured and executed in this way. Only then, when people were apt to forget the high price of salvation, did the crucifix become a standard part of Christian churches.

By the Middle Ages, these crosses, or "roods," became quite imposing and elaborate. Mounted on large screens in church sanctuaries, they hung amid flickering lamps and images of scenes from the Bible and the lives of the saints.

Today the crucifix may be suspended over the altar or fixed to the sanctuary wall. Or it may be carried in procession during the liturgy and installed by the altar. But it must be there, and it should be visible, so that Christians will not forget.

THE AMBO

AT A recent council, the Church spoke of having two tables in its worship: the table of God's word and the table of
Christ's body.[1] These tables are the altar (of course) and the
ambo. At the altar, the Church offers the Body of Christ.
At the *ambo,* the Church proclaims the word of the Lord.

The ambo is a lectern or pulpit used for the proclamation of the Sacred Scriptures. Sometimes these are very
simple structures. Sometimes they are very ornate. Always,
however, they are treated as something sacred, because

they are a place dedicated to reading God's inspired Scriptures. Just as the altar is used only for the Holy Sacrifice, so the ambo should be used exclusively for the reading of Scripture or other liturgical texts (the Easter Proclamation called the *Exsultet,* for example), for the preaching of the homily, or for announcing the prayer intentions during the universal prayer of the Mass.

In the ancient world, the Liturgy of the Word was an opportunity for people to encounter the Scriptures. There were no printing presses, computers, or photocopiers. The only way to disseminate a book was by copying it out by hand, a process that was very expensive and time-consuming—and minimally useful, too, since most people couldn't read.

Christians did not invent liturgical proclamation. Jesus himself observed it as a Jew attending synagogue. Saint Luke's Gospel (4:16–21) shows him on a Sabbath day reading from the scroll of the Prophet Isaiah, then interpreting the passage for the congregation. The words of the Old Testament were fulfilled in Jesus's proclamation. The story of that fulfillment, proclaimed to the world, would become the New Testament.

The Apostles continued the practice of liturgical reading, even as they established new forms of worship—sacramental forms. They wrote their letters to be read, along with the Old Testament books, in Christian worship. Saint Paul instructed his disciple Timothy: "attend to the public reading of Scripture, to preaching, to teaching" (1 Timothy 4:13; see also Revelation 1:3; Colossians 4:16; 1 Thessalonians 5:27). Proclamation is a powerful event, a solemn event. It is a ritual and liturgical event.

Indeed, from the earliest times, Christian worship has been divided into two halves: the Liturgy of the Word and the Liturgy of the Eucharist. Each half corresponds to rites associated with one of the Church's "tables." First, at the ambo, a priest, deacon, or lector proclaims the readings. "The dignity of the Word of God requires that in the church there be a suitable place from which it may be proclaimed and toward which the attention of the faithful naturally turns during the Liturgy of the Word" (GIRM 309). The ambo should be a permanent fixture, not movable, and positioned so that those who proclaim the word can be clearly seen and heard by the congregation.

Then, at the altar, the priest offers the Eucharistic prayer and the bread and wine become the Body and Blood of Christ. Thus, a certain pattern of proclamation and reception was built into the Church's ritual worship—and likewise into the design of Catholic churches. Because of the importance of the ambo and the altar, both are usually located within a church's sanctuary.

The *Catechism* explains that Christianity, unlike other religions, is not a "religion of the book," but a religion of the "Word" (CCC 108). Christ is God's living Word, now made flesh, and the Church proclaims the Word as Good News to the world.

When the Word is proclaimed, it is a moment of grace. The *Catechism* explains what happens at that moment by citing the story of Jesus's walk with two disciples on the road to Emmaus. Along the way, he "interpreted to them in all the Scriptures the things concerning himself," and then they knew him "in the breaking of the bread" (Luke 24:27, 35). To the early Christians, this was the outline of the Holy Mass: the breaking open of the Word followed by the breaking of the bread. It was the context that ensured the grace for understanding. The *Catechism* concludes: "If the Scriptures are not to remain a dead letter, Christ, the eternal Word of the living God, must, through the Holy Spirit, 'open [our] minds to understand the Scriptures' " (CCC 108; see also Luke 24:45).

Because of its holy purpose, the ambo is treated with great honor, and it should be built to inspire reverence. The U.S. Catholic bishops have asked that the two tables, ambo and altar, should bear a "harmonious and close relationship to one another in order to emphasize the close relationship between word and Eucharist."[2] The bishops have also asked that the ambo be built in an area large enough to accommodate a procession with the Book of the Gospels, with "a full complement of ministers bearing candles and incense."

The design of the church accommodates the rites of the Church as both give honor to the Scriptures. In the ancient churches, the priest or deacon would often be accompanied by attendants bearing candles or lamps. This was necessary for the sake of reading, because the churches were very dark. Today the Church retains the ceremony, even in churches with electric floodlights. Now the candles are more purely symbolic, signifying the light of Christ that goes out to the world by means of the Gospel proclamation. The incense signifies the "aroma of Christ" going out from the ambo "among those who are being saved" (2 Corinthians 2:15).

THE PRESIDER'S CHAIR

IT SEEMS an ordinary piece of furniture, but the U.S. Catholic bishops list the "chair of the priest celebrant" as one of "the principal ritual furnishings within the sanctuary," along with the altar and the ambo.[1] Its dignity requires that it be made with the same care as these other important furnishings.

At the time of the Lord's Incarnation, the chair or throne was a nearly universal symbol of teaching authority. Philosophers taught their disciples while seated in the chair that belonged to their office. Kings and emperors issued laws and edicts from a special throne. Jesus himself used such terms when he spoke of Judaism's chief teachers in his time: "The scribes and the Pharisees sit on Moses' seat; so practice and observe whatever they tell you" (Matthew 23:1). Their authority was abiding and God-given, even if their behavior disappointed him.

As we have said previously, the Greek word used in the Gospel to denote that "seat" of authority is *kathedra,* and it is the word the early Christians came to associate with the authority of their clergy. The North African Tertullian, writing in Latin, referred to the bishops' office as *cathedrae apostolorum*—the seats of the Apostles.[2] We still borrow from this usage today as we call a bishop's church his "cathedral." The cathedral takes its name from the seat of authority within its sanctuary.

Every church has a presider's chair, and that chair is a sign of the parish priest's authority, delegated to him by his bishop, whose own authority comes from Jesus Christ. The bishops are the successors of the Apostles, to whom Jesus said: "All authority in heaven and on earth has been given to me. Go therefore and make disciples of all nations, baptizing them in the name of the Father and of the Son and of the Holy Spirit, teaching them to observe all that I have commanded you" (Matthew 28:18–20). It is in the church that the clergy, today as in ancient times, baptize and teach, in fulfillment of Jesus's command.

In ancient times, the bishop preached not from a pulpit or ambo, but from his chair, where he remained seated. So important was this furnishing that the Church of Antioch in Syria from very early times celebrated a feast day dedicated to the Chair of Saint Peter. The Catholic Church still celebrates that feast today.

The fourth-century historian Eusebius makes the connection between the chairs occupied by the Apostles and the chairs belonging to the clergy of his day: "And in this temple there are also thrones. . . . On these rest those souls in which rest the Holy Spirit's gifts, which were in olden times seen by the holy Apostles."[3]

From apostolic times, the Church has been hierarchical. Christian worship respects this God-given division of labor, and it is reflected in the interior arrangement of churches. So explains the *General Instruction of the Roman Missal*: "The chair of the Priest Celebrant must signify his function of presiding over the gathering and of directing the prayer. Thus the more suitable place for the chair is facing the people at the head of the sanctuary" (GIRM 310).

Hierarchy in the Church is not like hierarchy in the world. It should not be about power or exploitation. Jesus, after all, told his inner circle: "If any one would be first, he must be last of all and servant of all" (Mark 9:35). Nevertheless, the office comes with a certain authority and dignity, and these are reflected in the symbolic chair. The U.S. Catholic bishops acknowledge that selecting the presider's chair requires a delicate balance: "The chair reflects the dignity of the one who leads the community in the person of Christ, but is never intended to be remote or grandiose."[4]

The presider's chair signifies an office bestowed by the sacrament of holy orders. Thus, this chair should be occupied by only ordained clergy—a bishop, priest, or deacon. If laypeople lead a prayer service, they should do so from a chair outside the sanctuary.[5]

CREDENCE TABLE

OFF TO the side in the sanctuary is a small piece of furniture called the *credence table*. It might be a freestanding piece of furniture or a ledge on a niche in the wall. On this surface rest the vessels (chalice and paten) and the elements

to be offered (bread, wine, and water), awaiting the time when they will be used in the Mass. Also kept there are the bowl, water, and towel the priest uses for washing his hands at the offertory of the Mass. The wine and water are usually kept in cruets. The unconsecrated wafers (called hosts) are kept in a special box. The chalice and paten, sometimes covered with their special cloths, may be kept on the credence table from the beginning of Mass until the offertory, when they are moved to the altar. If they are to be brought to the altar in an offertory procession, they will be kept elsewhere in the church, usually on a similar table, during the first part of the Mass.

The credence table may be attended by an altar server or deacon during the liturgy. The table's name derives from the Latin word *credens,* which means "believing." Its Italian equivalent, *credenza,* has entered the English language to describe any table or sideboard used in a home or other setting. Its origin is uncertain.

The table of the altar is reserved for sacrifice—exclusively for sacrifice. Only the elements to be offered (and their sacred vessels) should be placed on the altar during the Mass, and these should rest on the altar only when they are being offered. Until then, their proper place is the credence table, which thus plays a very practical and important role in preserving the sanctity of the altar.

DOMES AND SPIRES

CHRISTIANITY MAY be marginalized in political discourse, censored in the media, and bleached out in public-school history textbooks, but the Church's steadfast witness is evident to anyone who stands on a hill and surveys the roof tops of a small town. Against the horizon, above the signs for bakeries and groceries and hardware stores, stand the domes and spires and steeples of churches. They are visible even in city skylines, squeezed between skyscrapers. Atop the distinctive roof, inevitably, is a cross.

"A church tower is a beacon to direct the faithful to the house of God," said the nineteenth-century British architect August Welby Pugin.[1] He knew a bit about towers; he designed Big Ben, the clock tower on Westminster Palace in London. (He was also a fervid convert to the Catholic faith.)

The church's tower, he continued, "is a badge of eccle-

siastical authority, and it is the place from whence the heralds of the solemnities of the church, the bells, send forth the summons. Let no one imagine that a tower is a superfluous expense. It forms an essential part of the building, and should always be provided in the plan of a parochial church." Pugin went so far as to say that "a flat roof is contrary to every principle" of church building.

As a designer of great towers he may be forgiven his enthusiasm. A tower is not in fact "essential" to a church, but it has become a common element of churches, and for good reason: In the language of architecture, it teaches doctrine. A tower climbs heavenward; and if it terminates in a pointed spire, it positively points to heaven, indicating the direction of Christian worship. For Pugin, this "vertical principle" is "emblematic of the resurrection" of Christ: He rises up. It suggests also his ascension into heaven.

A *dome* is a raised semispherical structure atop a church. St. Peter's in Rome and Hagia Sophia in Constantinople are two famous domed churches. The inner structure of a dome is called the *cupola*. Seen from inside, it represents the arc of the sky—the heavens—so it is often decorated with images of the Blessed Trinity, the angels, and the saints. The cupola over the oldest church in Ravenna, Italy, the fifth-century Mausoleum of Galla Placidia, displays more than five hundred golden stars in a royal-blue sky, above white-robed Apostles and winged angels. It is a scene straight out of the heaven revealed in the biblical Apocalypse.

A cupola is sometimes the most fitting place to define the church's dominant theme. Around the base of the dome of St. Peter's Basilica in Rome are the words with which Jesus established the papacy in bestowing the office on Simon, son of John: "You are Peter, and on this rock I will build my Church. . . . I will give you the keys of the kingdom of heaven" (Matthew 16:18–19). Each letter is six and a half feet high, as tall as the average player in the National Basketball Association. St. Peter's was built during a time when the papacy was under an unprecedented attack. The architects wanted to make their message very clear.

The tops of the great churches reach up to heaven, but their names often refer back to Christianity's homey origins. The English word *dome* derives from the Italian *duomo,* which in turn comes from the Latin *domus,* meaning "house." The Italians often call a cathedral *il duomo,* because it is the house of God. Today's cathedrals are simply the great-grandchildren of the house churches founded by the Apostles, when they first taught the Gentiles to look up to heaven.

Even the grandest church is still a family home at heart. And even the humblest church houses a congregation aspiring to heaven. The towers, steeples, spires, and domes remind us of that.

Children have a nursery rhyme that shows the importance of these rooftop elements: "Here's the church; here's the steeple. Open the door, and see all the people." Perhaps Mr. Pugin was on to something. Towers and spires do raise the profile of the church against the city's skyline—and that's a very good thing, especially in a time when cultural elites would rather that the Church disappear.

BELLS

BELLS ARE the insistent and very public voice of the church, summoning the whole world to prayer. Churches are known by their bells, even by those who don't go to church. The sound of a bell, projected from a steeple or tower, gives a temporary air of sanctity to the surrounding streets. It intrudes into the grudges and vexations of distracted pedestrians. For laborers it provides a counterpoint to the sounds of power tools. Bells startle children at play and rouse sleeping dogs.

Bells are a dramatic device favored by poets and movie directors. They toll for the funeral of the fallen hero; they peal for the wedding of the happy couple.

They are the sacred background music of a parish's teeming life.

They are a customary, but not necessary, part of a church. The earliest churches, in fact, did not have them.

Living amid persecution, Christians did not want to draw attention to their worship, which was often held in secret. Only with the legalization of Christianity in AD 313 could the Church operate openly—and issue a public summons to worship. The first instruments used for that purpose were wooden clappers (common in the Eastern churches) and bells (more common in the West).

Over time, churches developed a system of customary times and tones for the ringing of bells. In the Middle Ages, a cathedral's bells could be a city's pride and joy. Bells were so revered that their blessing was called a "baptism." Each bell was given a distinctive name and even, sometimes, a coat of arms! The bells were often endowed by wealthy or noble families and engraved with prayers or lines from Scripture.

In many European villages, the church was the main civic building in town. Until fairly recently, few families owned clocks, and the church bells served as the measure of their days, ringing in the hours, half-hours, and even quarter-hours.

William Durand, the medieval bishop who wrote an extensive commentary on the parts of a church, dedicated an entire chapter of his work to bells.

Bells, he said, are to Christian worship what trumpets were to the worship of biblical Israel. They call God's people to worship. Demons flee when they hear church bells ringing. Bells are like preachers that exhort Christians to faith, he said.[1]

He explained, in minute detail, the symbolic meaning of every part of a bell: the bronze (fortitude), the clapper (the tongue of a learned teacher), the loop that holds the clapper to the bell (moderation), the wood of the frame (the cross of Christ), the rope (humility), and even the iron clamps that join the bell to the frame (charity). Every virtue that makes for a good bell, he said, makes for a good preacher.

There are certain traditional times for a Catholic church to ring its bells, though these vary widely depending on local custom (and zoning ordinances). The most common use of bells is as a "last call" to worship, issued shortly before Mass. Some parishes also ring the bells briefly at the beginning of the Eucharistic prayer, to let people nearby know that something momentous is about to happen. In places where the culture and population are strongly Catholic, you will sometimes see pedestrians make the sign of the cross at the sound of the bells.

Bells may also be rung at the traditional times for the Angelus prayers: most commonly at noon, but also at the sixth hour, both morning and evening. These prayers, a responsory with three Hail Marys, commemorate the Lord's Incarnation in the womb of the Virgin Mary. *The Angelus* by Jean-François Millet depicts the moment when two farmers hear the Angelus bell and interrupt their work to bow their heads in prayer.

The Church has, in various times and places, restricted the use of bells during certain seasons—during Lent and Holy Week, for example, periods that call for greater solemnity and austerity.

Traditionally rung by sacristans, church bells now are often powered by motors and timed by computers. In many places they have been replaced by recorded chimes played through a loudspeaker.

The purpose remains the same. Whether pealing joyfully or tolling mournfully, they call the world to prayer.

Inside the church, smaller bells (sacring bells) are sometimes used to signal the beginning of Mass and the consecration of the Eucharist. Like almost everything in the church, they hark back to Israel's Tabernacle and the Jerusalem Temple. There, the high priest wore vestments fringed with bells, which rang as he entered the Holy of Holies (see Exodus 28:33–35).

Today, when the bells ring, the Good News goes out for all to hear: "When Christ appeared as a high priest . . . he entered once for all into the Holy Place, taking not the blood of goats and calves but his own blood, thus securing an eternal redemption" (Hebrews 9:11–12).

DOORS

In some of the Eastern Churches, there is a point in
the liturgy when the deacon calls out, "The doors! The
doors!" To visitors, it seems a strange interpolation—a red

herring amid formulas of blessing. Why this sudden notice of the church's entryways?

This exclamation marks the point in the service when in ancient times the non-Christians were ushered outside, the doors were locked, and only faithful Christians remained inside. "Holy things for the holy!" is a later line, which explains the closing of the doors. Only those who receive Christ's life and holiness in baptism—and keep it faithfully—may approach the altar for Holy Communion.

Thus the doors were closed. The line remains in many liturgies, though the custom of expelling non-Christians and mortal sinners is no longer observed. The liturgy preserves the line because it reminds us of the distinction between the Church and the world. The spiritual writer Romano Guardini offered a twentieth-century perspective on the doors of a church.

> When you step through the doorway of a church you are leaving the outer-world behind and entering an inner world. The outside world is a fair place abounding in life and activity, but also a place with a mingling of the base and ugly. It is a sort of market place, crossed and recrossed by all and sundry. Perhaps "unholy" is not quite the word for it, yet there is something profane about the world. Behind the church doors is an inner place, separated from the market place, a silent, consecrated and holy spot. It is very certain that the whole world is the work of God and his gift to us, that we may

meet Him anywhere, that everything we receive is from God's hand, and, when received religiously, is holy. Nevertheless men have always felt that certain precincts were in a special manner set apart and dedicated to God.

Between the outer and the inner world are the doors.[1]

Father Guardini's distinctions are precise and important. The world is good; it is created by God, and it is his gift to the human race. Yet the world is not God. It can lead us to God. But he transcends it. We must learn to refer all things in the world to God, praising him for their goodness. To do that, we step apart now and then. We enter holy ground. We step through the doors of the church.

One of the early Christian commentators on the church, Saint Maximus the Confessor, dwelt lovingly on the meaning of the doors. He said: "The entrance of the people into the church . . . signifies not only the conversion of infidels to the true and only God, but also the amendment of each one of us who believe yet still violate the Lord's commandments."[2]

To pass through the doors of a church is symbolically to undergo a conversion—to accept God's invitation to change one's life. Saint Maximus continued: "The closing of the doors and the entrance into the holy mysteries . . . mean in general the passing away of sensible things and the appearance of spiritual realities and the new teaching of the divine mystery involving us and the future concord, unanimity, love and identity of everyone with each other and with God."[3]

To pass through the doors is symbolically to enter heaven, to pass into the presence of God, with all the saints and all the hosts of spiritual creatures: angels and archangels, thrones and dominions.

Separated by almost a millennium and a half, Father Guardini and Saint Maximus both want us to savor the moment of our entry into church.

The Christians who have built great churches have shared this intense awareness of the importance of the doors. Massive bronze doors stand guard before some of the Roman basilicas. At the ancient church of Santa Sabina in Rome, the wooden doors date back to the fifth century, and they are richly decorated with carvings of scenes from the Bible. At St. Peter's in Rome, one door is sealed, only to be opened for special times the pope designates as years of jubilee.

In times when Catholic culture was pervasive, the church's doors represented a place of safety—"sanctuary." Refugees and even criminals could run to the doors and hang on to the oversized loop handles. As long as they were there, they could claim immunity from harm, and there they would await the arrival of clergy to serve as their mediators and protectors. Law-enforcement officials were conscience bound, and even legally bound, to respect such claims to sanctuary.

The church is still a refuge of sinners. Even worshippers who have committed no crimes are still unworthy to enter the holy mysteries. For only God is truly holy. All human holiness is a grace, a sharing in divine life. Everyone who enters the door of a church is seeking sanctuary.

Jesus understood this, so he issued an invitation: "I am the door; if any one enters by me, he will be saved, and will go in and out and find pasture" (John 10:9).

HOLY WATER FONT

BAPTISM IS the ordinary way someone enters God's family, the Church. A typical Catholic church is constructed so that believers will remember their baptism every time they enter the building. Near the entryway will be a basin or bowl, the holy water font (sometimes called a *stoup*).

Some are small, and some are monumental—as in Europe's great cathedrals. Some have fountains of running water. Most, however, are humble and unimposing.

At the holy water font, Catholics dip their fingers and trace the form of a cross over their upper body.

It's an ancient practice, mentioned often in the writings of the early Church. Long before the faith was legalized in the Roman Empire, Christians everywhere were making the sign of the cross—in places as far-flung as North Africa, Egypt, Palestine, and Rome. We possess at least three sets of ancient prayers for the blessing of holy water.

As soon as it was legal to build churches, Christians built them and included holy water fonts—some of them quite elaborate. The Church historian Eusebius writes of one such building, at Tyre, whose entrance was marked with "symbols of sacred purifications" and "fountains that furnish an abundance of water so that those who come within may purify themselves."[1]

The practice has been enduring. The Church's *Catechism* says that the holy water font fulfills something important in the design of the church and the life of a Christian: "The gathering of the People of God begins with Baptism; a church must have a place for the celebration of *Baptism* (baptistry) and for fostering remembrance of the baptismal promises (holy water font)" (CCC 1185).

As with so many architectural traditions, this one has deep biblical roots. Solomon surrounded the Jerusalem Temple with many stations for ritual washings. People would cleanse themselves symbolically before approaching the Temple for prayer. The practice was domesticated in later times and observed at times of prayer, even in homes. When Saint Paul said, "I desire then that in every place the men should pray, lifting holy hands" (1 Timothy 2:8), he was probably referring to the practice of ritual washing before prayer.

For believers, water evokes the memory not only of their own baptism, but of so many manifestations of God's power, told and retold in the Scriptures: at the beginning of creation, God breathed upon the waters; Noah's family was rescued as floodwaters enveloped the earth; Moses split the waters of the Red Sea and then drew water miraculously from a desert rock; water flowed from the wounded side of Jesus Christ; and the book of Revelation shows "the river of the water of life, bright as crystal, flowing from the throne of God and of the Lamb" (Revelation 22:1).

At the entrance of a church, the holy water font recalls the Prophet Ezekiel's vision at "the door of the temple; and behold, water was issuing from below the threshold of the temple toward the east (for the temple faced east); and the water was flowing down from below the right end of the threshold of the Temple, south of the altar" (Ezekiel 47:1). For Catholics today, the Church is the temple of God's presence; and its waters purify, refresh, and renew.

An ancient text called the *Apostolic Constitutions* records a prayer of blessing over holy water and attributes it to the Apostle Saint Matthew. The prayer counts off many benefits of holy water: "the power to restore health, to drive away diseases, to banish demons, and to disperse all snares through Christ our hope."[2]

Holy water is a sacramental, a sacred sign that moves people to prayer and becomes an occasion of grace. The spiritual writer Romano Guardini wrote: "Therefore the Christian when he enters church moistens forehead, breast and shoulders, all his person, with the clean and cleansing water in order to make clean his soul."[3] It is a fitting way to enter the temple, the house of God: the church.

Many churches have, in addition to the holy water font, a holy water dispenser, usually with a valve or spigot so that worshippers can fill a small container for devotional use at home.

THE POOR BOX

FOR CHRISTIANS, care for the poor is not simply a kind thing to do; it is an act of worship. It is an integral part of the Church's ritual public worship, the liturgy. It is something done in church.

It has been so since the time of the Apostles. Saint Paul gives instruction for "the contribution" to be gathered on "the first day of every week," at Sunday Mass (1 Corinthians 16:1–2). This collection is to be used for "relief" of those in need (2 Corinthians 8:4).

It is a fundamental tenet of Christianity that God will judge people's lives based on their performance of bodily and spiritual "works of mercy." It's not enough merely to have vague good intentions. Have you fed the hungry, given drink to the thirsty, clothed the naked, and visited the imprisoned? Jesus put the matter to us in explicit terms:

"As you did it to one of the least of these my brethren, you did it to me" (Matthew 25:40).

Christians are faithful to this command in countless ways, but perhaps most effectively through the charitable works of the Church. On the parish level, these works are funded through the Sunday collection, as in the days of Saint Paul, but also through contributions—given in secret—to the church's poor box.

Poor boxes come in all shapes and sizes. They are usually kept locked and secured to the floor, wall, or some other surface, to safeguard them from theft. This money, after all, is kept in trust for the poor, whom Christ identified with himself.

In the first full century of Christianity, two authors, Tertullian and Saint Justin Martyr, gave somewhat extensive accounts of the Church's charitable work. Both authors did this not as part of a discussion of institutional works, but rather as part of their discussion of the Mass. If Christians are generous, it is because God has been supremely generous to them. In the Mass, God gives himself to them in the Eucharist. Christians, in turn, give as God gives. They give sacrificially, and they give from their substance, not their surplus. Saint Justin said that the contributions of Christians, in Rome in AD 150, took care of orphans, widows, the sick and needy, prisoners, and travelers. "In a word," he said, the Church "takes care of all who are in need."[1]

Tertullian said that his African Church, around AD 190, paid "to support and bury poor people, to supply the wants of orphan boys and girls, and of elderly people who are homebound; also, those who have suffered shipwreck; and those condemned to work in the mines, or banished to the islands, or shut up in the prisons." He concluded: "It is the deeds of a love so noble that lead many to put a brand upon us. 'See,' they say, 'how they love one another.' "[2]

It's not a noisy love. The poor box enables Christians to give quietly, anonymously, so that no one sees, yet generously. This is the way Jesus prescribed: "When you give alms, do not let your left hand know what your right hand is doing" (Matthew 6:3). He illustrated the principle by telling his disciples to observe a certain scene at the Jerusalem Temple. "He looked up and saw the rich putting their gifts into the treasury; and he saw a poor widow put in two copper coins. And he said, 'Truly I tell you, this poor widow has put in more than all of them; for they all contributed out of their abundance, but she out of her poverty put in all the living that she had' " (Luke 21:1–4).

The poor box is often hidden away toward the back of a place of worship. But the truly generous manage to find it. And Jesus sees.

THE SACRISTY

THE DRAMA of the Mass begins before the congregation sees the ministers. The drama begins "offstage," so to speak, in prayer, in the sacristy.

The *sacristy* (sometimes called a *vestry*) is the room in

the church where the clergy don their vestments and pre-
pare the sacred vessels for Mass. Most include ample closet
and cabinet space, so that these sacred items can be stored
properly and kept in the best condition. Since the chalices
and patens used in the Mass are made of precious metals,

they also require secure storage, to keep them safe from abuse and theft.

A sacristy is not a mere dressing room or storage room. It is a sacred space where the liturgy really begins.

Most sacristies include a crucifix among their decorations, to remind the priest of the action he is about to undertake. He is preparing to offer the Mass *in the person of Jesus Christ,* and the Mass will be a re-presentation of Jesus's once-for-all sacrifice of the cross.

Thus, when a priest vests for Mass, he unites himself with Christ and prepares himself for the offering. In a popular Easter hymn Catholics sing that Christ was "robed in flesh our great High Priest." A Christmas carol speaks of Christ as "veiled in flesh . . . the incarnate Deity." So a vesting priest imitates God's eternal Word putting on flesh for our salvation. Before every Mass he will symbolically "put on Christ" (Galatians 3:27) with his vestments.

It was once customary (but not obligatory) for a priest to say certain prayers while he put on each item of his vestments. Each item has a special symbolic meaning, established in the early Church, and this meaning is reflected in the "vesting prayers." The simple vesting prayers reflect deeply biblical notions found in both the Old Testament (see Exodus 28) and the New Testament (see Revelation 19:8). When a priest dresses for Mass, even today, in the third millennium, he is clothing himself in the garments of the first millennium. His liturgical wardrobe distinguishes him from the congregation and sets the sacred time of worship apart from the ordinary time of the streets and marketplace.

A priest's life is demanding, and his duties tend to follow him wherever he goes. As he enters the sacristy, he often finds himself among parishioners and other liturgical ministers. As a spiritual father, he must be attentive to them and treat them with respect, decorum, and kindness. But he should also do what he can to focus his mind and heart on the sacred mysteries he is about to celebrate. The Catholic Church urges this insistently in its documents. In a passage prescribing "sacred silence," the *General Instruction of the Roman Missal* says: "Even before the celebration itself, it is a praiseworthy practice for silence to be observed in the church, in the sacristy, in the vesting room, and in adjacent areas, so that all may dispose themselves to carry out the sacred celebration in a devout and fitting manner" (GIRM 45).

This appears also as a special concern of Pope Benedict XVI, who wrote: "Active participation in the eucharistic liturgy can hardly be expected if one approaches it superficially, without an examination of his or her life. This inner disposition can be fostered, for example, by recollection and silence for at least a few moments before the beginning of the liturgy."[1]

The Vatican Office for the Liturgical Celebrations of the Supreme Pontiff has offered practical and sensitive advice for priests who struggle to find this silence in their bustling parishes:

> The priest in a pastoral setting may struggle to establish the desired silence that the sacristy should

exemplify, especially at the times when he needs to greet and meet the faithful. For him, in particular, the texts of the preparation before Mass and of the thanksgiving afterwards offer wholesome thoughts to uplift the priest's mind and heart; and, in whole or in part, these can be prayed at any time. They also recognize human constraints on time and afford spiritual assistance rather than the imposition of any obligation on the priest, who is trying to celebrate Mass as reverently as he can. . . . It is desirable that a priest do what is possible to give time, even briefly, to enable spiritual preparation before Mass and an act of thanksgiving after the celebration has ended. He will feel strengthened for having done so.[2]

Within the sacristy is a special basin or sink called the *sacrarium,* which is used for pouring out the water remaining from the purification of sacred vessels and linens after Mass (see GIRM 334). The sacrarium empties not into a sewer, but rather directly into the earth, a more suitable destination for sacred things.

Referring to the contents of the chalice consecrated during the Mass, the *General Instruction of the Roman Missal* says: "If any of the Precious Blood is spilled, the area where the spill occurred should be washed with water, and this water should then be poured into the sacrarium in the sacristy" (GIRM 280). "The sacrarium also can be used to discard old baptismal water, left-over ashes, and the previous year's oils, if they are not burned."[3]

The sacristy is usually unseen, but it is a very important element in a church's design. It can set the tone for the Church's worship. The U.S. Catholic bishops observed: "Well designed, well equipped, and well organized sacristies contribute to the smooth function of the liturgy."[4]

THE CHOIR

THE MASS has inspired many of the greatest works of music by history's greatest composers: Bach, Beethoven, Mozart, Haydn, Liszt, Schubert, Bruckner, Puccini, Verdi, Dvořák . . . continuing into the modern era with jazz settings by Dave Brubeck and Mary Lou Williams.

Yet even the greatest music is beside the point. The point of the church is the Mass, and the Church's music must serve the Mass—by glorifying Christ in a beautiful and memorable way.

Since the music serves the liturgy, most churches include areas for a choir or musicians, but these people are positioned to be heard and not necessarily seen. Sacred music is written to be prayed, not performed.

The word *choir* refers to the area reserved for this ministry. In the oldest churches it was an area close to the sanctuary, as "choir" members belonged to the order of clergy; in some churches today the choir is still somewhere around the sanctuary. Today the choir may be a loft—a gallery or upper level—above at the back of the church or along the sides. A choir may also be located in one or both of the church's transepts.

Since liturgical singing is not a performance, the choir's place is not a stage. According to the U.S. Catholic bishops, "ministers of music are most appropriately located in a place where they can be part of the assembly and have the ability to be heard." When they must be placed near the sanctuary, "the placement of the choir should never crowd or overshadow the other ministers in the sanctuary nor should it distract from the liturgical action."[1]

Music has always played an integral part in biblical religion. The book of Psalms is the people of Israel's hymnal for divine worship. The Old Testament gives us vivid accounts of music in the Temple liturgy. For example:

> [King Hezekiah] stationed the Levites in the house of the Lord with cymbals, harps, and lyres. . . . The Levites stood with the instruments of David, and the priests with the trumpets. Then Hezekiah commanded that the burnt offering be offered on the altar. And when the burnt offering began, the song to the Lord began also, and the trumpets, accompanied by the instruments of David king of Israel. The whole assembly worshiped, and the singers sang, and the trumpeters sounded; all this continued until the burnt offering was finished.

When the offering was finished, the king and all
who were present with him bowed themselves and
worshiped. (2 Chronicles 29:25–29)

Music was integrated in Israel's liturgy and led the people
to profound adoration: they bowed and worshipped.

In the New Testament, the Apostles continued the
practice of using music in the liturgy. More than once,
Saint Paul exhorted his congregations to praise the Lord
with "psalms and hymns and spiritual songs" (Ephesians
5:19 and Colossians 3:16). The early Christians took up
these forms with gusto, and pagan outsiders identified the
Church's worship with its distinctive music. In AD 111, a
Roman governor named Pliny, a persecutor of the Church,
observed that the Christians in his region would meet on
Sunday "before dawn and sing responsively a hymn" be
fore partaking of "ordinary and innocent food."[2] An early
tradition records that Saint Ignatius of Antioch, a contem
porary of the Apostles, introduced antiphonal singing into
the church after he had a vision of the angels singing that
way in heaven.[3]

Many of the early Church Fathers were great promot-
ers of liturgical music. Saint Ephrem of Syria composed
hymns to the Blessed Virgin and the Holy Eucharist and
organized choirs for his churches. Saint Ambrose did the
same in Milan, as did Saint Basil in the land now known as
Turkey, and Saint Hilary in what is now France. Saint Basil
said: "Who can consider as an enemy one with whom he
has sung God's praises with one voice? Singing the psalms

imparts the highest good, love, for it uses communal sing-ing, so to speak, as a bond of unity, and it harmoniously draws people to the symphony of one choir."[4]

Saint Augustine, writing in North Africa in the fourth century, confessed that he loved liturgical music, and he recognized the role it played in his own conversion.[5] He wished the music to be the best that it could be. Yet he also recognized a danger in its goodness: If it veered into per-formance, it could distract worshippers from their worship and turn a congregation into a mere audience.

The choir has a great purpose within the larger plan of a church. For centuries the builders of churches have struggled to balance the concerns of saints and pastors like Augustine: maximizing beauty for God's sake, and in such a way that beauty is offered on the altar, not made an end in itself. In the precision with which the great architects have placed the choirs in churches, we see their love of beauty, but their greater love for God.

CANDLES

LIGHTS, LAMPS, candles, fire have always served as ritual signs of God's presence. When Moses first experiences the nearness of the Lord, it is at the burning bush; and the Lord God tells Moses he is standing on holy ground. When Moses receives instructions for the decoration of Israel's sanctuary, the Tabernacle, he is told to make the Menorah, a seven-branched golden lampstand, which would light up the Holy of Holies (Exodus 25:31–40). It is no accident that the Menorah resembled nothing so much as a burning bush. It would serve as a permanent reminder of God's appearance to Moses—and a permanent sign of the divine presence in the Tabernacle. When Solomon built the Temple in Jerusalem, he commissioned "ten golden lampstands . . . and set them in the temple, five on the south side and five on the north" (2 Chronicles 4:7). These remained in place until they were taken as plunder by the Babylonians (see Jeremiah 52:19), and the resulting darkness was a sign of God's absence.

Light is the sign of God's presence, and the Gospel describes the Incarnation as a most brilliant and enduring blaze. Jesus Christ identifies himself saying, "I am the light of the world; he who follows me will not walk in darkness, but will have the light of life" (John 8:12). Thus, light signifies a living presence. It is alive. Indeed, its life and light are identical: "In him was life, and the life was the light of men. The light shines in the darkness, and the darkness has not overcome it" (John 1:4–5).

Inevitably, early Christian worship was suffused with light—with lights, lamps, candles, fire. Saint Luke reports that when the Apostle Paul celebrated Mass at Troas, "there were many lights in the upper chamber where we were gathered" (Acts 20:8). It was clearly overkill. To have so many lamps in a small space was not only superfluous, but it robbed the room of oxygen, with disastrous results (see verse 9).

Yet the people lit "many lights" as a fitting sign of the Lord's abundant presence—his Real Presence.

Beyond the apostolic era, the early Fathers testify to the devotional lighting of lamps, not only at Mass, but also at the tombs of the martyrs. For God is always with his saints. Saint Jerome said, in AD 406: "All those who light these tapers have their reward according to their faith."[1]

Still today—and for all the same reasons—a Catholic church is a well-lighted place. What illumines it? The flickering flames of altar candles, the paschal candle, the sanctuary lamp, and votive lights.

Candles are an important part of the altar's furnishing. The *General Instruction of the Roman Missal* specifies that "on or next to the altar are to be placed candlesticks with lighted candles: at least two in any celebration, or even four or six, especially for a Sunday Mass or a holy day of obligation, or if the Diocesan Bishop celebrates, then seven candlesticks with lighted candles" (GIRM 117).

Votive lights are usually smaller candles placed, sometimes in great quantity, before images of Jesus, the Blessed Virgin, or the saints. Votive candles are a sign of homage, and they represent the abiding prayers of the faithful people who lit them.

The *sanctuary lamp* is a "special lamp which indicates and honors the presence of Christ." The Church's canon law specifies that this lamp "is to shine continuously before a tabernacle in which the Most Holy Eucharist is reserved" (CIC 940). The lamp may be "fueled by oil or wax," and "should shine permanently to indicate the presence of Christ and honor it" (GIRM 316).

The *paschal candle,* or Easter candle, is a large candle blessed at the Easter Vigil liturgy and used that day in the blessing of baptismal water. It is used in the liturgies throughout the Easter season and all year round at baptisms and funerals. In a rite that dates back to the ancient church, as the priest holds this candle aloft on Holy Saturday, he chants, "Christ our light," and the people respond, "Thanks be to God." Saints Augustine and Jerome speak of the paschal candle. It is usually the largest candle in the church, and it symbolizes the pillar of cloud and pillar of fire that led the Israelites on their sojourn in the desert. It can be massive indeed. According to one source, at Rome's Basilica of St. John Lateran, the candle used "was so lofty that the deacon was wheeled in a portable pulpit to light it."[2]

The paschal candle is usually decorated with a cross, the Greek letters alpha and omega, and the numerals of the current year; it is embedded with five grains of incense, representing the five wounds of Christ.

The U.S. Catholic bishops wax poetic on the paschal candle: "The paschal candle is the symbol of 'the light of Christ, rising in glory,' scattering 'the darkness of our hearts and minds.' "[3]

It is a longstanding tradition to make church candles— entirely or mostly—out of beeswax. Each candle stands for Christ: the beeswax for his flesh, the wick for his soul, the flame for his divinity. The ancients held that only wax drawn by bees from flowers could purely represent the flesh that Christ received from his Virgin Mother. While the use of beeswax candles is customary, it is not required. The bishops say, simply, that candles for liturgical use should be made of material that provides "a living flame without being smoky or noxious." In the same breath, in order to "safeguard authenticity and the full symbolism of light," they forbid the use of "electric lights as a substitute for candles."[4]

Everything about a candle proclaims Christ's presence in the church. Joy is the inevitable corollary to that presence. The bishops tell us that candles "are signs of reverence and festivity."[5] Saint Jerome delighted in the fact that the Church lit candles even when there was ample light in the building. "Whenever the Gospel is to be recited, lights are brought forth, even if it's at noontime—not, certainly, to drive away darkness, but to manifest a sign of joy."[6]

Where the presence of God is palpable, joy will abound, and there will be many candles burning. "Then," says the Seer, "I turned to see the voice that was speaking to me, and on turning I saw seven golden lampstands, and in the midst of the lampstands one like a Son of man" (Revelation 1:12–13).

"And the city has no need of sun or moon to shine upon it, for the glory of God is its light, and its lamp is the Lamb" (Revelation 21:23).

THE AMBRY

THE CHRISTIAN faith is ever ancient and ever new, to borrow a phrase from Saint Augustine. As time passes, the Church develops a deeper understanding of what God has revealed to the world in Jesus Christ. Unfortunately, there is a downside: as Christians are drawn into doctrinal and theological reflections, they can lose touch with the original and ordinary meanings of basic terms.

At the root of Christianity is *Christ,* which most people think of as simply a part of Jesus's name. It is not, however. It is a title, meaning "anointed," a direct translation of the Hebrew word *moshiach,* Messiah. Israel's kings and priests were anointed in rites that initiated them into their sacred offices. They could be called simply the Lord's "anointed" (see Psalm 2:2). In this, they prefigured Jesus, the King of Kings and the great high priest, who is simply called "Christ."

At the root of Christianity, then, is an anointing—an application of oil—and that is the business of a parish church's *ambry*.

The ambry is a repository for the three different oils used in the Church's sacramental rites. The *Catechism* explains: "The *sacred chrism (myron)*, used in anointings as the sacramental sign of the seal of the gift of the Holy Spirit, is traditionally reserved and venerated in a secure place in the sanctuary. The oil of catechumens and the oil of the sick may also be placed there" (CCC 1183).

The word *ambry* has workaday origins. It comes from the same Latin word from which we derive the word *armory,* and that Latin word, *armarium,* was often used to describe a laborer's toolbox. The oils and chrisms kept in the ambry are the tools of the Church's trade, so to speak.

Ambries take a wide variety of forms—a cabinet or a rack or simply a niche in the wall. They should be stable and secure, to prevent spillage, theft, or other abuse. Since oil is particularly sensitive to light and temperature, churches usually keep their ambry in a place that is relatively dark and cool. In cathedral churches, ambries can be quite large, to house larger quantities of the oils.

The bishop blesses the three sacramental oils once a year, at the Chrism Mass during Holy Week (usually during the day on Holy Thursday). This Mass commemorates Jesus's establishment of the sacramental priesthood at the Last Supper. When the bishop blesses the oils, they are in large containers, and after the Mass they are dispensed in smaller vessels and taken out to the parishes of the diocese.

A parish replenishes its supply at that time, and any oil remaining from the previous year is either burned up or poured into the ground by way of the church's sacrarium (a special sink for the proper disposal of sacred things).

As he distributes the oils, the bishop symbolically renews his connection with every parish in the diocese. Through those oils he takes part in thousands of sacramental events throughout the year. He is there with the priest at the deathbed of a parishioner. He is there with the deacon who receives babies into the parish church at baptism. He is there to welcome adult converts, who are confirmed on Easter Vigil. In all these sacraments, the clergy apply the oils. They anoint. They make *Christians,* true to the root meaning of the word.

Historians say that the first recorded extraction of olive oil appears in the Hebrew Bible, and that oil was extracted for use in the liturgy: for ritual anointing and for fuel for the lamps. Jesus did not abandon these practices when he instituted the New Covenant. We read that his first disciples "anointed with oil many that were sick and healed them" (Mark 6:13). The Apostle James asks his readers: "Is any among you sick? Let him call for the elders of the Church, and let them pray over him, anointing him with oil in the name of the Lord" (James 5:14). Saint John mentions the place of anointing in the sacraments of initiation: "You have been anointed by the Holy One," and "the anointing which you received from him abides in you. . . . His anointing teaches you about everything" (1 John 2:20, 27).

The ambry is a repository of the Church's great supernatural resources: oils that heal, strengthen, empower, and illumine—oils that are used for anointing, in rites that bestow the office of Christ and convey the life of Christ.

RELICS AND RELIQUARIES

MOST CHURCHES have relics somewhere. Usually they're hidden away, in the altar. Sometimes, however, they're displayed openly in a *reliquary*.

Relics include the physical remains of a saint and objects that have touched a saint's body. Christians have honored such items since biblical times; indeed, this practice set Christians apart from all their neighbors. In the ancient world, both pagans and Jews held that contact with a dead body rendered a person ritually unclean. The anti-Christian Roman emperor Julian the Apostate complained that Christians had polluted the cities by filling them with tombs.

The Christians were undeterred by his taunts and continued their practice of devotional visits to the catacombs and pilgrimages to the tombs of the Apostles.

They had biblical reasons for doing so. They read the

New Testament and saw that "God did extraordinary miracles by the hands of Paul, so that handkerchiefs or aprons were carried away from his body to the sick, and diseases left them and the evil spirits came out of them" (Acts 19:11–12). If God sent such power through Paul's handkerchief while the Apostle walked the earth, how much more power and grace would flow through his relics, preserved and honored by the Church, now that he is in heaven?

Christians discerned this power at work in the Old Testament as well. When a dead man was hastily cast into the grave of the Prophet Elisha, "as soon as the man touched the bones of Elisha, he revived, and stood on his feet" (2 Kings 13:21).

The book of Revelation either describes contemporary Christian practice or sets the agenda for future Christian practice when it shows us "under the altar the souls of those who had been slain for the word of God and for the witness they had borne" (Revelation 6:9). Probably the earliest reliquaries were the altars and shrines built over the relics of the saints.

This loving practice of preserving relics is evident in the earliest account of martyrdom produced after the New Testament. In the middle of the second century, the Christians of Smyrna wrote about the execution of their aged bishop, Saint Polycarp, who had been a disciple of the Apostle John. After Polycarp's death, the Christians "took up his bones, which are more valuable than precious stones and finer than refined gold, and laid them in a suitable place. There the Lord will permit us to gather ourselves together, as we are able, in gladness and joy, and to celebrate the anniversary of his martyrdom."[1]

Reliquaries come in many different shapes and sizes, sometimes depending on the size of the relics they contain. They can be caskets, altars, small pyxes, ornamental crosses, ostensoria similar to the monstrance used for exposition of the Blessed Sacrament.

Indeed, some of the grandest churches are outsized reliquaries. The Basilica of St. Peter in Rome was built to glorify God, but also to house the mortal remains of the man whom God chose to be the Prince of the Apostles.

A church's relics can range in size and significance. They might include a small chip of bone or even a complete skeleton. Parts of a saint's body are known as "first-class relics" or "primary relics," and only first-class relics should be kept in or under a church's altar. Items that have come into physical contact with a saint's body—such as articles of clothing or a piece of fabric that has been touched to a saint's bones—are called "second-class" or "secondary relics." These, too, may be venerated in a church, though they are usually not kept in or under the altar. (A separate category of relics includes the very few items preserved from Our Lord's suffering and death: wood from the True Cross, and so on.)

Keeping relics is a practice that harks back to the origins of Christianity, but it's not an anachronism. The Church's canon law states, "The ancient tradition of placing relics of martyrs or other saints under a fixed altar is to be preserved" (CIC 1237 §2). The *General Instruction of the Roman Missal* affirms: "The practice of the deposition of relics of Saints, even those not Martyrs, under the altar to be dedicated is fittingly retained. However, care should be taken to ensure the authenticity of such relics" (GIRM 302).

SYMBOLS AND ABBREVIATIONS

CHRISTIANS IN all places and in every age share a common visual language. When twenty-first-century pilgrims visit the third-century catacombs in Rome, they see and recognize symbols that adorn the walls of their parish churches back home. This language has an abundant vocabulary, and scholars have compiled dictionaries and even multivolume encyclopedias of Christian symbols. In the following pages we offer brief definitions of the symbols and abbreviations most commonly used in church decoration.

There is another type of visual symbol often found in churches. Sometimes an artist or artisan will take a small detail from a biblical narrative and use it to represent the entire story. A nail or a crown of thorns, for example, will be used to represent all of Jesus's sufferings (see Matthew 27:29). A basket of loaves and fishes will signify Jesus's miraculous feeding of the multitude (see John 6:1–13). There are far too many of these symbols to mention. The Bible is a library of many books; and each book is filled with stories; and each story is filled with small details that have been rendered in art.

Some devotional phrases from the first centuries of Christianity have been abbreviated and passed down as design elements. Often they are preserved in their original languages, Greek and Latin. Some of these are "decoded" below.

At the end of the chapter is a key to the symbolic values of numbers used in decoration.

> *Anchor.* Hope (see Hebrews 6:19–20); the anchor's shape is suggestive of the cross.

> *Ankh.* An Egyptian "looped cross," representing the crucified Jesus. Also a symbol of Christ's life-giving sacrifice.

> *AΩ.* Alpha and omega, the first and last letters of the Greek alphabet, representing God as the beginning and the end (see Revelation 1:8).

> *Chalice with Snake.* Saint John the Evangelist. According to an ancient tradition, John was once

given a poisoned cup. After he said a blessing, the poison departed in the form of a snake. The snake is also a symbol of wisdom (see Matthew 10:16).

Chi-Rho. The letter *X* superimposed upon the letter *P*; in Greek, these are the initial letters of the word for Christ.

Circle. God's eternity. Interlocking circles represent the sacrament of marriage, in which "two become one" (see Matthew 19:5).

Cloud. God's glory and presence (see Exodus 40:35).

Crown. The kingship of Jesus. Also martyrdom as a share in Christ's Kingship (see Revelation 2:10).

Dove. God the Holy Spirit, the Third Person of the Blessed Trinity (see John 1:32).

Eagle. Saint John the Evangelist, whose Gospel begins by soaring to heaven ("the Word was with God") then swoops to earth in the Incarnation ("the Word was made Flesh"). (See Revelation 4:5–7 for the symbols for the four evangelists.)

Eye. God the Father, all-knowing and all-seeing.

Fire. The Holy Spirit (see Acts 2:3).

Fish. A symbol of Jesus. In Greek, the initials of the words for "Jesus Christ, Son of God, Savior" yield the word ΙΧΘΥΣ (fish); the symbol evokes Eucharistic images in the Gospel (John 6:11, 21:13).

Fleur-de-lis. The lily, signifying the Blessed Virgin Mary, totally pure.

Grapes. The wine offered in the Eucharist, the Blood of Christ.

Hand. God the Father, all-powerful.

Heart. The Sacred Heart of Jesus (see John 19:34) or the Immaculate Heart of Mary (see Luke 2:19, 35).

Host and Chalice. The Eucharist.

IC XC. An abbreviation for the name of Jesus Christ; sometimes appears with the word *Nika,* meaning "conquers" or "is victorious."

IHS. The first three letters of the name *Jesus* in Greek; also an abbreviation for the Latin *In Hoc Signo,* the command heard by the emperor Constantine when he had a vision of the cross: "By this sign you shall conquer."

INRI. The initials of the Latin title that Pontius Pilate ordered to be placed on the cross (see John 19:19). It means "Jesus of Nazareth, the King of the Jews."

Keys. The papacy; the first pope, Saint Peter, to whom Jesus gave the keys to the Kingdom (Matthew 16:19).

Lamb. Jesus, called "the Lamb of God" by Saint John the Baptist (John 1:29) and throughout the Book of Revelation; often shown with wounds "as though it had been slain" (Revelation 5:6).

Lamp. Jesus, the "light of the world" (see John 9:5).

Lion. Saint Mark the Evangelist, whose Gospel begins with John "crying in the wilderness," like a lion (see Revelation 4:5–7 for symbols of the four evangelists).

Moon. The Blessed Virgin Mary, who appears mystically as "a woman . . . with the moon under her feet" (Revelation 12:1).

MP ΘY. Abbreviation for the Greek words for "Mother of God," always associated with the Blessed Virgin Mary.

Olive Branch. Peace.

Orb and Cross. Jesus's Kingship over the world.

Ox. Saint Luke the Evangelist, whose Gospel emphasizes the Temple liturgies of sacrifice; the ox was a common sacrificial animal (see Revelation 4:5–7 for symbols of the four evangelists).

Peacock. Jesus's glorified body. When the peacock displays its plumage, it is transfigured (see Luke 9:29).

Pelican. The Eucharist. The ancients believed that the mother pelican drew blood from her breast to feed her young.

Phoenix. The legendary bird that dies in flames and rises from ashes. A symbol of Jesus risen from the dead.

Rainbow. God's covenant with the human race, renewed with the family of Noah (see Genesis 9:13).

Rose. The Blessed Virgin Mary, who gave roses to Saint Juan Diego at Guadalupe.

Seashell. Saint James. Pilgrims to his shrine in Spain picked up shells along the way.

Shepherd. Jesus, the "Good Shepherd" (John 10:14).

Shepherd's Staff. The office of bishop (see Jeremiah 3:15).

Ship. The Church; Saint Peter's fishing boat; Noah's ark.

Skull and Crossbones. Death. If shown beneath the cross, they represent Calvary, "place of a skull" (John 19:17). They also represent Adam, whose sin brought death (1 Corinthians 15:22). According to legend, Calvary was Adam's burial place.

Stars. Sometimes represent angels (see Revelation 8:12); sometimes Jesus (Revelation 22:16). The six-pointed star represents King David and his royal lineage, including Jesus, "Son of David."

Sun. Jesus, the "sun of righteousness" (Malachi 4:2).

Tree. The Garden of Eden; life and knowledge. The cross.

Triangle. The Blessed Trinity, three Persons in one God.

Trumpet. God's judgment (see Revelation 1:10).

Vine. Jesus (see John 15:1, 5). If shown with grapes, also a symbol of the Eucharist.

Water. Baptism; the Holy Spirit (see Revelation 22:1).

Wheat. Jesus's Real Presence in the Eucharistic hosts (see John 12:24, 6:35).

Winged Man. Saint Matthew the Evangelist, whose Gospel emphasizes Jesus's human ancestry (see Revelation 4:5–7 for symbols of the four evangelists). Also, an angel.

1—The oneness of God; the uniqueness of Jesus and the Christian way: "one Lord, one faith, one baptism" (Ephesians 4:5). A church ordinarily has one main altar and one tabernacle.

2—The two natures of Christ, human and divine. Also the Bible's two testaments, Old and New.

3—The Trinity, the three Persons in the Godhead: Father, Son, and Holy Spirit.

4—The Gospels: Matthew, Mark, Luke, and John.

5—The wounds of Christ, in his hands, feet, and side.

7—The days of creation; completion, holiness. The lights in the Menorah in the Jerusalem Temple.

8—The superabundance of God's grace. Easter was sometimes called the Eighth Day, because it was one day beyond the Sabbath. Many baptismal fonts have an octagonal shape.

9—The Trinity (nine is three threes); the orders of angels.

10—The Commandments of God (Exodus 20:1–17).

12—The Apostles; the tribes of Israel.

SACRED IMAGES

CHRISTIANS HAVE not ceased using words because Jesus is God's definitive Word. (This book, like all Christian books, is filled with words.) Nor do Christians hesitate to use images because Jesus is the definitive "image of the invisible God" (Colossians 1:15). Jesus is *the* Word, and he is *the* image (in Greek, *eikon*; icon). He gives meaning to

the religious discourse of Christians. He is resplendent in
Christian devotional art.

Catholics are known for their sacred art. Many of the
greatest works in history are housed not in museums, but
in churches. And many of the works of art that are now
in museums once adorned churches—and were created to
inspire worship.

The art in churches takes many forms in many
media—from fabric to mosaic, fresco to bronze. Sometimes images hang or stand in nooks, niches, or side chapels. Sometimes they adorn the sanctuary's furnishings:
relief sculptures may appear on an altar, for example, and
scriptural scenes are often cast on the golden doors of a
tabernacle.

The subject matter, too, is as richly varied, as diverse as
the stories of the Bible and as multicultural as the lives of
the saints. Sacred art can be figurative or abstract, manner-
ist or realistic. Ethiopians have one way of making icons;
Greeks have another.

Sacred art is as multiform and abounding as the created
world that it reflects and elevates to the glory of God.

At a few times in history, misguided teachers have
questioned whether it was proper for Christians to honor
images. In the eighth century a Byzantine emperor fell
under the influence of a rising religious movement, Islam,
which placed an absolute prohibition on representational
art, whether sacred or secular. This emperor, Leo III, forbade the making of icons and ordered the churches to be
purged of them—even those that were already hundreds
of years old. His soldiers gathered them up and burned

them in enormous bonfires. If devout Christians held fast to their images, the soldiers hacked off their hands and threw those into the bonfire as well. It is no exaggeration to say that Catholics are attached to their tradition of devotional art; they have defended it with life and limb.

The act of destroying images marked a clear break with the tradition of Christian worship. Even by the eighth century Christians had already filled the world with churches—and those churches were filled with images. Before Christianity was legal, the walls of the catacombs were crowded with art, including images depicted on the lamps and medals that could be found in the dust of those underground shrines.

In every age, iconoclasts—the word means, literally, "picture smashers"—will cite the first commandment as their authority. God told Moses: "Since you saw no form on the day that the Lord spoke to you at Horeb out of the midst of the fire, beware lest you act corruptly by making a graven image for yourselves, in the form of any figure, the likeness of male or female" (Deuteronomy 4:15–16).

The Church Fathers responded, as always, with the "incarnational principle," the Catholic Thing. They said that the "Word became flesh" (John 1:14)—and that God's enfleshment changed everything. Saint John of Damascus explained: "In other ages God had not been represented in images, being bodiless and faceless. But since God has now been seen in the flesh, and lived among men, I represent that part of God which is visible."[1]

The *Catechism* offers variations on the same theme, making many careful distinctions.

The Christian veneration of images is not contrary to the first commandment which proscribes idols. Indeed, "the honor rendered to an image passes to its prototype," and "whoever venerates an image venerates the person portrayed in it." The honor paid to sacred images is a "respectful veneration," not the adoration due to God alone. (CCC 2132)

Sacred images in our churches and homes are intended to awaken and nourish our faith in the mystery of Christ. Through the icon of Christ and his works of salvation, it is he whom we adore. Through sacred images of the holy Mother of God, of the angels and of the saints, we venerate the persons represented. (CCC 1192)

Christian iconography expresses in images the same Gospel message that Scripture communicates by words. Image and word illuminate each other. (CCC 1160)

When sacred images portray Jesus Christ, they are portraying God (again, see Colossians 1:15). When they depict the saints and angels, they are expressing God's grace and glory. These subjects merit the best art that can be produced; and indeed they have inspired the masterworks of history's greatest artists. Think of Michelangelo's *Pietà* and *Last Judgment*. Think of Leonardo's *Last Supper*. The *General Instruction of the Roman Missal* says:

The Church constantly seeks the noble assistance of the arts and admits the artistic expressions of all

peoples and regions. In fact, just as she is intent on preserving the works of art and the artistic treasures handed down from past centuries and, in so far as necessary, on adapting them to new needs, so also she strives to promote new works of art that

are in harmony with the character of each succes-
sive age. (GIRM 289)

The Incarnation expands the limits of artistic representation, and it pushes the boundaries of every style. It
forces the most talented painters and sculptors to confront
ultimate matters.

Sacred art points beyond itself, to heaven, which
touches earth in the sanctuaries of Catholic churches.

> In the earthly Liturgy, the Church participates,
> by a foretaste, in that heavenly Liturgy which is
> celebrated in the holy city of Jerusalem, toward
> which she journeys as a pilgrim, and where Christ
> is seated at the right hand of God; and by venerat-
> ing the memory of the Saints, she hopes one day to
> have some share and fellowship with them.
>
> Thus, in sacred buildings images of the Lord,
> of the Blessed Virgin Mary, and of the Saints . . .
> should be displayed for veneration by the faithful
> and should be so arranged so as to lead the faith-
> ful toward the mysteries of faith celebrated there.
> (GIRM 318)

The blind men who followed after Jesus begged him,
"Lord, let our eyes be opened" (Matthew 20:33). These
words could serve as a prayer for everyone who is confronted with sacred art, because the art in churches requires a different kind of vision—not the critical faculties

of an aesthete or an art historian, but the gaze of a disciple. Pope Benedict XVI called all who enter churches to open their eyes in this way: "The profound connection between beauty and the liturgy should make us attentive to *every work of art* placed at the service of the celebration."[2]

STATIONS OF THE CROSS

THE "WAY of the Cross" is commemorated in fourteen "stations" along the walls of a church, usually marked by images, but sometimes by simple crosses and Roman numerals.

The devotion began long ago. It may have started with eyewitnesses of Jesus's suffering and death. Those who remained in Jerusalem would likely have retraced the Lord's footsteps and guided fellow believers along the Way, quietly telling the story as they walked. Once the course was mapped out, it was passed down through the generations by word of mouth. Members of the local church preserved the memory and shared it. Every year curious and devout Christians made pilgrimages to the Holy Land—stealthily during the persecutions, more openly from the fourth century onward—and in the streets of Jerusalem they walked the Way. The Jerusalem liturgy of

Holy Week memorialized the events of Jesus's Passion. On Holy Thursday, the city's bishop led the procession from the Garden of Gethsemane to Calvary.

Pilgrims took the custom home with them; and there, in the churches of Europe, they memorialized the stops along the Way, with images and special prayers or meditations. In the fourteenth century, the pope entrusted the holy sites to the Franciscan order, and these friars zealously promoted the Way of the Cross as a popular expression of devotion to the Lord's Passion.

These became known by the Latin title *Via Crucis,* the "Way of the Cross." They are also called the *Via Dolorosa,* the "Mournful Way." They are always described as a *Via*—a Way, a Road—a revisiting of Jesus's winding pathway through Jerusalem's streets.

In churches the Way is marked out in stations in various forms. One parish in Pittsburgh features fourteen side chapels with life-sized carved-wood figures in tableaux. Most parishes have simpler images, painted or sculpted, often in bas-relief, on numbered plaques. Some consist of no more than a number and a cross. Whether statuary or plaques, the stations are placed at intervals, so that those who follow them are walking a "way" along with Jesus. Since the eighteenth century the stations have been considered almost standard equipment in a church building.

Christians may pray the Way alone or in groups, silently contemplating the scenes or using one of the many sets of meditations authored by the saints. The set written by Saint Alphonsus Liguori in the eighteenth century remains very popular, but there are many others. It has become customary for the popes to write or commission new meditations every year for their observance of Good Friday in Rome's Colosseum.

Though the practice of this devotion was widespread in the Middle Ages, the number and sequence of stations varied from place to place. Eventually, popular piety settled on these fourteen scenes, drawn from scriptural accounts and oral traditions about the sufferings of Jesus.

1. Jesus is condemned to death.
2. Jesus carries the cross.
3. Jesus falls the first time.
4. Jesus meets his sorrowful Mother.
5. Simon of Cyrene helps Jesus carry the cross.
6. Veronica wipes the face of Jesus.
7. Jesus falls the second time.
8. Jesus meets the women of Jerusalem.
9. Jesus falls the third time.
10. Jesus is stripped of his garments.
11. Jesus is nailed to the cross.
12. Jesus dies on the cross.
13. Jesus's body is taken down from the cross.
14. Jesus is laid in the tomb.

Christians in every age are drawn to this devotion. In a very graphic way, the Stations of the Cross depict the power of sin. Jesus accepted the cross and took on the sins of every human being. Spiritual tradition holds that Jesus fell three times under the weight of the cross and got up each time to continue his sorrowful way to Calvary, the Crucifixion, and our redemption.

Every human being bears the weight of crosses fashioned by their own personal sins; and without God's grace no one would be able to get back up after each fall. Only the grace of God's forgiveness extends the helping hand that lifts believers up from failure, fault, and sin and allows them to continue their journey to God.

The Way of the Cross is a path to walk in response to Jesus's invitation: Those who wish to come after him, he says, must deny themselves, take up their cross, and follow (Mark 8:34–35).

STAINED GLASS

Perhaps the earliest precursors of motion picture photographers were the builders of the great medieval cathedrals. They created images that were invisible to the surrounding world, yet spectacularly beautiful to worshippers inside the church. Catching sunlight, the bits of glass seem to coalesce and come alive, revealing the forms of standing saints in heavenly splendor.

The windows provide motion pictures, really: the images change slightly as the earth slowly makes its rounds and clouds pass now and then before the sun.

Colored glass was used to decorate churches as far back as the fourth century. But stained glass as we know it came into use only with the technological advances of the twelfth and thirteenth centuries. From the monasteries of Europe came a providential convergence of artistic vision and the science of chemistry. Mixing organic materials,

ash, and river sand, the monks produced glassy jewels of every shape and color—to catch the sun, reflect it, refract it, and magnify it in churches large and small. Some of the windows that were created were epic in scale, telling stories in multiple images. Some were an explosion of color surrounding small framed scenes.

Making stained glass is an expensive process, and labor-intensive. Over time, cash-strapped parishes found ways to "cheat" and simulate the effects of stained glass by painting clear glass. Again, it was an artistic method that arose with developments in technology—this time, translucent paints that could hold up under a daily onslaught of the elements. Many North American parish churches of the early twentieth century, built by struggling immigrants, have windows of this type.

The windows in St. Patrick's Cathedral in New York City were fashioned using Old World methods and are worthy to be ranked with those of the finest of France's High Gothic churches. Pope Benedict praised the stained glass at St. Patrick's during his 2008 visit to the United States and drew spiritual lessons from their "flood" of "mystic light."

> From the outside, those windows are dark, heavy, even dreary. But once one enters the church, they suddenly come alive; reflecting the light passing through them, they reveal all their splendor. Many writers . . . have used the image of stained glass to illustrate the mystery of the Church herself. It is only from the inside, from the experience of faith and ecclesial life, that we see the Church as she truly is: flooded with grace, resplendent in beauty, adorned by the manifold gifts of the Spirit. It follows that we, who live the life of grace within the Church's communion, are called to draw all people into this mystery of light.[1]

The figures in stained glass are idealized, never realistic. They represent the glorified bodies of persons in heaven. The images are rich in symbolic detail. The saints hold items associated with their work or, in the case of martyrs, their death.

The second-century bishop Saint Irenaeus of Lyon said that "the glory of God is man fully alive, and the life of man is the vision of God. If the revelation of God through creation already brings life to all living beings on the earth, how much more will the manifestation of the Father by the Word bring life to those who see God."[2]

Each window suggests how God reveals himself through creation. The sun, like divine light, brings life to the creatures sketched out in glass. In kaleidoscopic color Christians see the saints—those who see God—transformed by the heavenly vision. Fully alive, the saints glorify God, and so do the windows that depict them.

MARY

SOMEWHERE IN every Catholic church will be an image or symbol of the Blessed Virgin Mary. Her presence has always, from the beginning, marked off a church as Catholic. Some of the oldest Christian images we know —in the Roman Catacombs and in the Fayoum in Egypt—are images of Mary.

Unless she is depicted with her divine Son, she is not usually front and center, but she is given a prominent place nonetheless. Such placement reflects her importance in the redemption of fallen humanity. When she received word that she was to bear the Messiah, she was an unknown girl in a no-account village in a remote province at the edge of the Roman Empire. Yet by saying yes at the Annunciation she achieved an utterly unique place in the history of salvation.

All over the world, on every inhabited continent, there

are shrines, churches, chapels, and oratories dedicated to
Mary. In many countries the principal shrine recalls an
apparition of Mary to the people of that land. Every land
honors her as a special intercessor, and she stands as their
patroness with an astonishing visibility.

It is not a visibility she sought. When she received the
visit from the angel Gabriel, she protested that she was
nobody important. She was a "handmaiden" of "low es-
tate" (Luke 1:48). When she heard the Lord's plan for her,
however, even she had to admit that "henceforth all generations will call me blessed." And the members of the
Church in every generation have done so.

They bless her memory with murals, canvases, mosaics,

icons, statues, bas-relief, stained glass, tapestries, wood-work, stencil, and ceramic.

Sacred images tell the story of salvation; and it is difficult, if not impossible, to tell the story of salvation without assigning the Blessed Mother a prominent place. The conception of the Lord, upon which rested our salvation, depended upon her consent. She gave birth to Jesus and nursed him, attended by angels and by wise men from distant lands. She nourished and taught Jesus through his childhood and adolescence. She accompanied him as he launched his public ministry and performed his first miracle at the Wedding at Cana, transforming water into wine. She remained with him when almost everyone else abandoned him, and she stood beneath his cross. When he had risen, the disciples gathered around her as they awaited the outpouring of the Holy Spirit at Pentecost. The book of Revelation shows her with Jesus in heaven. There she is an icon of the Church, crowned with glory.

When Saint Paul wished to summarize Jesus's life and significance in just a single line, he found it impossible to tell the story without mentioning Mary: "But when the time had fully come, God sent forth his Son, born of woman, born under the law" (Galatians 4:4). When the Church retells the story—in its creeds and in its preaching—she is always there. And so she is in our churches as well. When sacred art recounts the events of Jesus's life, it is not simply the story of one man. When the Word became flesh, he took that flesh from the substance of a mother, from *his* mother, the mother he had chosen from all eternity.

In each house of worship, the U.S. Catholic bishops write, "it is particularly desirable that a significant image of the patron of the church be fittingly displayed, as well as an image of Mary, the Mother of God, as a fitting tribute to her unique role in the plan of salvation."[1]

Her role is singular, essential, but not central. At the center of Catholic devotion is Mary's Son, Jesus Christ, to whom she remains ever near.

> The special and unique dignity of the Mother of God has been expressed in the devotional art of the Church. Artists have painted her image in wondrously meditative fashion as a sign of sure hope and solace for the pilgrim People of God. At the same time, veneration of Mary, like that of all other devotions, leads clearly to the worship of her Son. The location, style, and importance of Marian images in the church demonstrate the intimate connection she has with the Eucharistic liturgy of Christ, as well as its distinctions.[2]

Thus, everyone who enters a Catholic church will encounter the mother as they encounter her Son. Sometimes she is represented by an image, sometimes more simply by her initial *M,* by a symbol (such as a rose or a fleur-de-lis pattern), or even by the color traditionally associated with devotion to her (blue).

Where Jesus is, there is Mary; and, as at Pentecost, so today: There the Church gathers.

THE BAPTISMAL FONT

FOR A Christian, the baptismal font is where spiritual life begins.

The Eucharist is the sacrament of sacraments and the primary reason for the building of churches, but baptism grants a person *access* to the Eucharist. Baptism is the sacramental prerequisite for participation in all the other sacraments. The Church's law commands: "Every parish church is to have a baptismal font" (CIC 858 §1).

Today most of those who are baptized are infants born into (or adopted by) Christian families. The rite takes place at the *baptismal font,* in an area of the church called the *baptistery.* The baptismal font is an ornamental basin that should accommodate the baptism of both babies and adults. The baptismal font may vary widely in shape and size. Sometimes the font is a pool in which an adult can be immersed. Sometimes it is a smaller receptacle, fixed

in place and usually made of stone. The baptistery may be a chapel within a larger church, a freestanding building, or simply the corner of the sanctuary where the font has been placed.

The font should hold a prominent place, because of its

importance in the life of the Church. Baptism is the gateway to the Eucharist, and many churches are designed to reflect this "integral relationship between the baptismal font and the altar."[1] Sometimes church designers manifest this relationship by lining up the two areas along the same "architectural axis." Sometimes the association is established by the use of the same or similar materials in both places. The important thing is that "the baptismal font and its location reflect the Christian's journey through the waters of baptism to the altar."[2]

As with the Eucharist, so with baptism: Christians have always been deeply concerned with doing it right, even when in the past they often had to work with serious contraints. In the early years of the Church, as we have seen, Christians worshipped where they could, and they were baptized as they were able. The Church's oldest sacramental manual, known as the *Didache,* dates from the first century and allows for a range of ritual possibilities: "Having first said all these things, baptize 'in the name of the Father, and of the Son, and of the Holy Spirit,' in running water. But if you have no running water, baptize in other water; and if you cannot do so in cold water, do so in warm. But if you have neither, pour out water three times upon the head 'in the name of Father and Son and Holy Spirit.' "[3]

Note the careful repetition of the words of the formula, which Jesus himself revealed to the Apostles (see Matthew 28:19). Note also the flexibility for accommodating a variety of circumstances. These guidelines reflect a time when the Church owned few (or no) church buildings and Christians had to make do with whatever was at hand.

Yet, as soon as Christians had opportunities, they built structures for baptism, just as they built structures for the Holy Mass. In the town of Dura-Europos, in Syria, an intact church survives from the early third century, and within it are distinct rooms for baptism and for celebrating the Eucharist.

During those early centuries, at least in some places, most of the candidates for baptism were adult converts from Judaism and paganism. At Dura-Europos, the sacrament involved partial immersion in a pool in the floor of the baptistery chamber.

After the legalization of Christianity came the construction of the great basilicas. Many of these included not just a church, but also a campus of ancillary buildings, the most prominent of which was a freestanding baptistery chapel. Christians built the fonts or pools in these buildings—and often the entire building itself—as eight-sided structures. The number eight had sacred connotations. Jews considered the Sabbath, the seventh day of the week, to be holy. The day after the Sabbath—the day when Jesus rose from the dead—could be counted either as the first day of the week or the eighth, suggesting a superabundance of holiness. Since baptism is traditionally an Easter sacrament, an octagonal font suited the occasion. Also the early Christians believed that salvation through baptism had been prefigured by Noah's ark, in which eight people were saved (see 1 Peter 3:18–22).

These associations led Saint Ambrose, in the fourth century, to draw up a descriptive dedication for a new baptistery in Milan, Italy.

Eight-sided is the lofty shrine to match its sacred use;
Eight-angled is the font to show its benefits profuse;
With such a number grace and life supplanted human guilt
And with such number must the hall of baptism be built.[4]

In the nineteenth and twentieth centuries there was a great renewal of interest in the study of ancient Christianity, and many architects took pains to imitate the structures used by the early Church. Many of the baptismal fonts currently in use are octagonal or have some octagonal elements.

Freestanding baptisteries, however, declined in use after the sixth century. By then, most of the peoples of the West had embraced Christianity. There were few non-Christian adults remaining to convert. Most of the new Christians baptized were small babies, and baptisteries began to be located in smaller rooms or nooks inside main churches.

The current norms prescribe that baptistery areas should be "large enough to accommodate a good number of people," and that they should also house the church's paschal candle, so that it can be used in the rite of baptism and so that the sacrament may be always associated with Easter.[5]

These associations become especially poignant at the other end of earthly life. In the rite of Christian burial, the casket is draped in fabric suggestive of a baptismal garment and it is sprinkled with water. The prayers speak of the deceased person's baptism. The U.S. Catholic bishops recommend "that there be a physical association between the baptismal font and the space for the funeral ritual."[6]

"What we call the beginning," said the poet T. S. Eliot, "is often the end. . . . The end is where we start from."[7] Nowhere is this truth embodied more clearly than in the baptistery of a Catholic church.

THE CONFESSIONAL

A BOOTH in the shadows, with screens and a promise of
absolute secrecy, the confessional has served as a setting for
countless dramas—on stage, in films, in novels, poems,
and memoirs.

The confessional's unassuming placement and design belie its God-given power to overcome shame, guilt, and sin with grace, peace, and forgiveness.

According to the *Catechism,* confessionals are among the three main sacramental areas in an ordinary church. The other two are the baptismal font and the altar. The confessional is the ordinary way station between the other two. The sacrament of reconciliation renews the cleansing of baptism, and it prepares the soul once again for Holy Communion. The *Catechism* states, "The renewal of the baptismal life requires *penance.* A church, then, must lend itself to the expression of repentance and the reception of forgiveness, which requires an appropriate place to receive penitents" (CCC 1185).

Confessionals vary in shape, size, and construction. In some, the priest sits inside a booth, behind a screen, receiving penitents who come forward, one at a time, to a kneeler outside in front. Another type of confessional places the priest and penitent in booths that are separated by a fixed screen. In some churches the "confessional" might be an open space with a chair and a kneeler, or two chairs separated by a screen.

The outside of some confessionals is equipped with a light to let people know when the room or booth is occupied, and when the priest is ready to see another penitent.

The screen, or grille, or "fixed grate," is the constant in every confessional. It is the one item that canon law requires (CIC 964 §2)—the element that ensures the anonymity of the penitent.

The proper place for a priest to hear sacramental confessions is in church (see CIC 964 §1). In the United States, according to the bishops' guidelines, a confessional should have a screen, but also some space must be set aside to "allow for confession face-to-face for those who wish to do so."[1]

A church's confessionals should be in a place that is "clearly visible" and "truly accessible" yet should also afford a measure of privacy. At the same time, the confessional should be as soundproof as possible.[2] So placement can be tricky.

Jesus gave his clergy the "power of the keys." He conferred on them the ability to forgive sins, a power that had formerly belonged only to God. First he gave the authority to Saint Peter. Later he gave it to the other Apostles, using the same words he had spoken to Peter: "Truly, I say to you, whatever you bind on earth shall be bound in heaven, and whatever you loose on earth shall be loosed in heaven" (Matthew 18:18; see also 16:19).

Later, after he had risen from the dead, Jesus gave the Apostles the grace they would need to carry on the superhuman task of forgiving sins: He said to them: " 'Peace be with you. As the Father has sent me, even so I send you.' And when he had said this, he breathed on them, and said to them, 'Receive the Holy Spirit. If you forgive the sins of any, they are forgiven; if you retain the sins of any, they are retained' " (John 20:21–23).

In that short address we learn a lot about the sacrament of Confession. It is a means of restoring peace. It is an essential part of the Church's mission to the world. It is accomplished through the power of the Holy Spirit. And its discipline is entrusted to human beings who have been called to a life of service to Jesus Christ.

The Apostle Saint Paul assumed all of the conditions of this sacrament when he rendered judgment and dispensed mercy to his churches (see, for example, 1 Corinthians 5:3–5). He spoke of his own work as a "ministry of reconciliation" (2 Corinthians 5:18).

The Church's rite of forgiveness is known by many names, which are used interchangeably: the *sacrament of conversion,* the *sacrament of penance,* the *sacrament of confession,* the *sacrament of forgiveness.* Each name highlights some particular aspect of what happens in the confessional.

In this sacrament, as in all the sacraments, God accommodates human weakness. The Church anticipates the fears, and the psychological and spiritual impediments, of its members, which might keep people away, and strives to overcome them in advance—by ensuring privacy and anonymity, by promising lifelong secrecy, and by making God's mercy abundantly available.

Modern people may take mercy for granted, but it is not a quality that came naturally to humanity. Many advanced pre-Christian cultures saw mercy as a defect, a sign of weakness. To them, the idea of a merciful god was an absurdity, an oxymoron. Divinities, after all, were supposed to be powerful, not weak, and power was made manifest in domination.

Christianity took the biblical message of mercy and self-giving love to the wider world, and one important way the Catholic Church has delivered the message has been by means of the confessional. Penance was at the heart of the life of the early Christians, and was the subject of some of their fiercest debates. Some wanted the Church to be a hotel for saints, not a hospital for sinners; they argued that the Church should place strict limits on the sins that could be forgiven—how many and how often. This group, the party of severity, argued that believers should have only one chance at reform in a lifetime—one chance to go to confession. After that, any future sins should exclude the sinner from Holy Communion forever—or at least until death was imminent.

The Church, guided by the saints, ruled in favor of greater mercy, and as a result, today there are confessionals visible and accessible in every parish church. Wherever Christians believe devoutly, confessionals are put to good use.

THE TABERNACLE

As Jesus walked toward Emmaus with his disciples, the time drew near for them to go their separate ways. But, Saint Luke recounts, "they constrained him, saying, 'Stay with us, for it is toward evening and the day is now far spent.' So he went in to stay with them" (Luke 24:29). The climax of the story is when he was "known to them in the breaking of the bread" (Luke 24:35).

The Incarnation is not merely a historical event. It is a present reality. The key is in the Greek of Saint John's statement: "And the Word became flesh and dwelt among us" (John 1:14). The English word *dwelt* is less evocative than the Greek original, *eskenosen,* which can be rendered "pitched his tent (*skene*) among us" or "tabernacled among us."

In a Catholic church, the *tabernacle* is the place of Jesus's abiding presence. It is the place where Eucharistic hosts, consecrated during the Holy Mass, are reserved.

The U.S. Catholic bishops write: "The reservation of the Eucharist was originally intended for the communion of the sick, for those unable to attend the Sunday celebration, and as Viaticum for the dying."[1] As early as AD 155 we find references to the practice of taking communion to the homebound. Through those years of persecution, when Christians met mostly in family homes, the Church Fathers gave careful instructions for reservation of the Blessed Sacrament. Their concern shows their reverence, and their reverence manifests their deep faith in the Eucharist. The consecrated bread must be reserved because it is Christ; and Christ must be adored because he is God (see CCC 1418). Thus the place where the Blessed Sacrament is kept is by nature a place of worship.

Already in the time of the Fathers, there arose the

practice of keeping the Eucharist in a sealed, secure, and suitably noble repository. Even in those early centuries, tabernacles varied widely in form. Some were mere *pyxes,* small containers made of precious metal or stone or ivory. Sometimes the pyx was cast in the form of a dove and suspended above the altar, a custom that became widespread in the Middle Ages. In later years, and especially in large churches, tabernacles were made to monumental size—in fact, they were called *sacrament towers*—so that their presence was not swallowed up by the vast interior space. The beauty and size of the tabernacle ensured that members of the congregation were always aware of its importance.

The English word *tabernacle* comes from the Latin *tabernaculum,* which in the Old Testament denotes the portable sanctuary of the people of Israel. For the Chosen People, the Tabernacle was the place of the presence. For the Catholic Church, the place of presence is still called the tabernacle.

Every parish church must have one (and only one) tabernacle; and canon law requires that "the church in which the Most Holy Eucharist is reserved is to be open to the faithful for at least some hours every day so that they can pray before the Most Blessed Sacrament" (CIC 937).

The tabernacle should be situated " 'in a most worthy place with the greatest honor,' " says the *Catechism* (1183). Church law further requires that the place be "distinguished, conspicuous, beautifully decorated, and suitable for prayer" (CIC 938 §2; see also GIRM 314).

The tabernacle should be both beautiful and secure. Its shape and size are not as important as its inviolability.

"The tabernacle in which the Most Holy Eucharist is reserved habitually is to be immovable, made of solid and opaque material, and locked in such a way that the danger of profanation is avoided as much as possible" (CIC 938 §3; see also GIRM 314).

Inside the tabernacle, the sacred hosts are kept in a pyx or ciborium and renewed frequently. Only the Blessed Sacrament may be reserved in a tabernacle.

In keeping with tradition, "near the tabernacle a special lamp, fueled by oil or wax, should shine permanently to indicate the presence of Christ and honor it" (GIRM 316). In most American churches, this light, often called the *sanctuary lamp,* is a candle, prominently placed and large enough to be seen.

The tabernacle is an element that sets a Catholic church apart from any other place on earth. The tabernacle makes the church the "tent" of God's abiding presence.

Canon lawyers are known for their practicality and for the plainness and precision of their prose; but the most eminent among them—at the Vatican's Pontifical Council for the Interpretation of Legislative Texts—spoke in ardent language recently, when they considered the dignity, placement, and security of the tabernacle.

> Christ's faithful are to hold the blessed Eucharist in the highest honor. . . . Indeed, in our age marked by haste even in one's personal relationship with God, catechesis should reacquaint the Christian people with the whole of Eucharistic worship, which cannot be reduced to participation in Holy Mass and to

receiving Communion with the proper dispositions, but also includes frequent adoration—personal and communal—of the Blessed Sacrament, and the loving concern that the tabernacle—in which the Eucharist is kept—be placed on an altar or in a part of the church that is clearly visible, truly noble and duly adorned, so that it is a center of attraction for every heart in love with Christ.[2]

EXIT

ALFRED HITCHCOCK was famous for the brief "cameo" appearances he made in his own movies. In the movie *I Confess,* about a parish priest, he appears as the first man in a horde rushing out of church as the doors swing open. We need not be as eager as that to leave our churches. But leave we must.

This book has many chapters, but not a word about overnight accommodations. Churches are homes, but not residences. Christians go to church for respite, not refuge.

Believers have always spoken about their churches with a certain ambiguity. They are proud of the buildings, the artwork, the achievement. And yet, kneeling in the cavernous interior of a Gothic cathedral, they are inspired also with an overwhelming awe, a fear of the Lord.

The church is home to Christians; it is heaven's settlement on earth, and yet it unsettles them, too. Long centuries ago, Saint John Chrysostom warned his congregation about feeling too cozy in church. He wanted them to cultivate a profound sense of reverence and observe the decorum proper to God's household. He wanted them to be mindful of the presence Moses encountered at the burning bush. He wanted them to feel what Jacob felt when he "was afraid, and said, 'How awesome is this place! This is none other than the house of God, and this is the gate of heaven' " (Genesis 28:17).

For a church is indeed the house of God and the gate of heaven. The statement is more true of the homeliest Catholic parish than it was of the burning bush or the ladder of angels. In a Catholic church, all heaven descends to fill the sanctuary. Christ himself reigns from the altar and from the tabernacle.

Churches are built for the sake of their altars, and their altars are built for the sake of the Mass. The Mass is celebrated for the glory of Jesus Christ—and to fulfill his people's need. The Martyrs of Abitina, North African believers of the early fourth century, spoke truly when they told their interrogator: "We cannot live without the Mass." One Sunday they gathered in their church, exposing themselves to certain danger, because they could not stay away. They could not live without their hour in the House of the Lord. They were prepared to die rather than miss a single Sunday.

A Catholic's hour at church, today as in the fourth century, ends in a mysterious way. It ends abruptly after

Communion, with a line that almost forces the congregation to the door. The concluding line in Latin is: *Ite, missa est.* In English it is: "Go forth, the Mass is ended."

From that short, sharp dismissal, in fact, we get the word *Mass* (Latin *Missa*). (And we also get the word dis*miss*al.)

Catholics love to go to church. The devout would love to linger there. But, really, it's all about being "sent forth by God's blessing." The dis*miss*al is a co*miss*ioning. Catholics leave church on a *miss*ion.

The ancients understood this well, so they called the Holy Eucharist "wayfarer's food." It is strength for the journey. Communion with Christ is grace the congregation takes in—in order to take it out with them, take it home, take it to work, take it to market. Abiding in the Christian, Christ encounters the world, as the world encounters Christ. God's holiness is contagious. By contact with Jesus, the dead rose to life, lepers were made clean, the blind came to see. That's the power the church still gives to Christians, the power they take out to the world—the world God wills to catch his holiness and become his holy temple.

Notes

Love Is the Builder
1. Saint Augustine, *Confessions* 13.24.
2. Dante, *Paradiso* 33.145.
3. Saint John of Damascus, *On the Divine Images,* part I.

What Is a Church?
1. Josef Pieper, *Problems of Modern Faith* (Chicago: Franciscan Herald Press, 1985), 97.
2. Jerome Murphy-O'Connor, O.P., *St. Paul's Corinth: Texts and Archaeology* (Collegeville, MN: Liturgical Press, 2002), 195–96.

What Is *the* Church?
1. Hugh of Saint Victor, *The Mystical Mirror of the Church* 1.
2. *Dedication of a Church and an Altar* (Dublin: Veritas, 1989), 15.
3. Quoted in Otto von Simson, *The Gothic Cathedral* (Princeton, NJ: Princeton/Bollingen, 1962), 8.

Mysteries of the Church
1. *Shulchan Aruch, Orach Chaim* 94.1, based on *Mishnah Berakhot* 30a.
2. Flavius Josephus, *Antiquities of the Jews* 3.7.

3. Otto Von Simson, *The Gothic Cathedral* (Princeton, NJ: Princeton/Bollingen, 1962), 11.
4. Tertullian, *On Baptism* 12.7.
5. *Apostolic Constitutions* 2.57.
6. See Joseph C. Plompe, *Mater Ecclesia: An Inquiry into the Concept of the Church as Mother in Early Christianity* (Washington, D.C.: Catholic University of America Press, 1943).

The Shape of a Church

1. See Saint Basil the Great, *On the Holy Spirit* 27. See also Joseph Cardinal Ratzinger, *The Spirit of the Liturgy* (San Francisco: Ignatius Press, 2000), chapter 3.
2. Eusebius, *Church History* 10.4.22.
3. Saint Clement of Rome, *To the Corinthians* 40.5 and 41.1.
4. Saint Maximus the Confessor, *Mystagogy* 3.

Churches and Other Worship Spaces

1. *Epistle of Barnabas* 15.8.

The Sanctuary

1. Eusebius, *Church History* 10.44.

The Nave

1. William Durand, *Rationale Divinorum Officiorum* 1.9.
2. Saint Maximus the Confessor, *Mystagogy* 3.
3. See Second Vatican Council, *Lumen Gentium,* Dogmatic Constitution on the Church (November 21, 1964), 34.

The Altar

1. Josef Pieper, *Problems of Modern Faith* (Chicago: Franciscan Herald Press, 1985), 102–3; see CCC 1383 and GIRM 296.
2. Saint John Chrysostom, *Homilies on 2 Corinthians* 20.3.
3. Saint John Chrysostom, *First Homily on Pentecost.*
4. Saint Irenaeus of Lyon, *Against Heresies* 4.18.6.
5. Eusebius, *Church History* 10.68.

Pews and Kneelers

1. United States Conference of Catholic Bishops (hereafter USCCB), *Built of Living Stones: Art, Architecture, and Worship* (Washington, D.C.: USCCB, 2001) § 85.
2. Ibid., § 86.
3. Second Vatican Council, *Sacrosanctum Consilium,* Constitution on the Sacred Liturgy (December 4, 1963), 14.
4. USCCB, *Built of Living Stones* § 86.

The Crucifix

1. Josephus, *Jewish War* 7.203.
2. USCCB, *Built of Living Stones: Art, Architecture, and Worship* (Washington, D.C.: USCCB, 2001) § 91.
3. Margaret Visser, *The Geometry of Love: Space, Time, Mystery, and Meaning in an Ordinary Church* (New York: North Point Press, 2000), 1.

The Ambo

1. See Second Vatican Council, *Dei Verbum,* Dogmatic Constitution on Divine Revelation (November 18, 1965), n. 21, *Mane Nobiscum,* no. 12 (2004).
2. USCCB, *Built of Living Stones: Art, Architecture, and Worship* (Washington, D.C.: USCCB, 2001) § 61–62.

The Presider's Chair

1. USCCB, *Built of Living Stones: Art, Architecture, and Worship* (Washington, D.C.: USCCB, 2001) § 55.
2. Tertullian, *The Prescription Against Heretics* 36.
3. Eusebius, *Church History* 10.66.
4. USCCB, *Built of Living Stones* § 63.
5. Ibid., § 116.

Domes and Spires

1. August Welby Pugin, *The Present State of Ecclesiastical Architecture in England* (London: Charles Dolman, 1843), 17–18.

Bells

1. William Durand, *Rationale.*

Doors

1. Romano Guardini, *Sacred Signs* (St. Louis: Pio Decimo Press, 1956), 37–38.
2. Saint Maximus the Confessor, *Mystagogy* 9.
3. Ibid., 24.

Holy Water Font

1. Eusebius, *Church History* 10.40.
2. *Apostolic Constitutions* 8.4.29.
3. Romano Guardini, *Sacred Signs* (St. Louis: Pio Decimo Press, 1956), 47.

The Poor Box

1. Saint Justin Martyr, *First Apology* 67.
2. Tertullian, *Apologeticum* 39.

The Sacristy

1. Pope Benedict XVI, Post-Synodal Apostolic Exhortation, *Sacramentum Caritatis* (February 22, 2007), 55.
2. Office for the Liturgical Celebrations of the Supreme Pontiff, *"Il silenzio in chiesa e in sagrestia prima e dopo la celebrazione,"* undated, on website Vatican.va (unofficial translation).
3. USCCB, *Built of Living Stones: Art, Architecture, and Worship* (Washington, D.C.: USCCB, 2001) § 236.
4. Ibid., § 234.

The Choir

1. USCCB, *Built of Living Stones: Art, Architecture, and Worship* (Washington, D.C.: USCCB, 2001) § 90.
2. Pliny the Younger, *Letters* 10.
3. Socrates Scholasticus, *The Ecclesiastical History* 6.8.
4. Saint Basil the Great, *Homilies on the Psalms* 1.2.
5. Saint Augustine, *Confessions* 10.33.50.

Candles

1. Saint Jerome, *Against Vigilantius* 7.
2. August Welby Pugin, *Glossary of Ecclesiastical Ornament and Costume* (London: Henry G. Bohn, 1844), 47.
3. USCCB, *Built of Living Stones: Art, Architecture, and Worship* (Washington, D.C.: USCCB, 2001) § 94.
4. Ibid., § 93.
5. Ibid., § 92.
6. Saint Jerome, *Against Vigilantius* 7.

Relics and Reliquaries

1. *Martyrdom of Polycarp* 18.2–3.

Sacred Images

1. St. John of Damascus, *Against Those Who Decry Sacred Images*, 1.16.
2. Pope Benedict XVI, Post-Synodal Apostolic Exhortation, *Sacramentum Caritatis* (February 22, 2007), 41; emphasis added.

Stained Glass

1. Pope Benedict XVI, Homily, St. Patrick's Cathedral, New York, April 19, 2008.
2. Saint Irenaeus of Lyon, *Against Heresies* 4.20.7.

Mary

1. USCCB, *Built of Living Stones: Art, Architecture, and Worship* (Washington, D.C.: USCCB, 2001) § 138.
2. Ibid., 157.

The Baptismal Font

1. USCCB, *Built of Living Stones: Art, Architecture, and Worship* (Washington, D.C.: USCCB, 2001) § 66.
2. Ibid.
3. *Didache* 7.
4. Quoted in Robert Milburn, *Early Christian Art and Architecture* (Berkeley, CA: University of California Press, 1988), 206.

5. Vatican Congregation for Divine Worship, *Rite of Christian Initiation of Adults* [RCIA] (January 16, 1988), General Introduction, n. 25.
6. USCCB, *Built of Living Stones* § 111.
7. "Little Gidding," in *Four Quartets;* T. S. Eliot, *The Complete Poems and Plays: 1909–1950* (New York: Harcourt, Brace, 1952), 144.

The Confessional

1. USCCB, *Built of Living Stones: Art, Architecture, and Worship* (Washington, D.C.: USCCB, 2001) § 103.
2. Ibid., § 103–105.

The Tabernacle

1. USCCB, *Built of Living Stones: Art, Architecture, and Worship* (Washington, D.C.: USCCB, 2001) § 70.
2. Pontifical Council for the Interpretation of Legislative Texts, "Safeguarding the Bread of Life Come Down from Heaven," June 4, 1999. See also Brian John Welding, *The Place and Site of Eucharistic Reservation in Current Legislation* (Rome: Pontifical University of Saint Thomas, 2002).

For Further Reading

Documents of the Church

All are available online at the websites of the Vatican (www.Vatican.va) and the United States Conference of Catholic Bishops (www.USCCB.org).

Built of Living Stones: Art, Architecture, and Worship. Washington, D.C.: USCCB, 2006.

Catechism of the Catholic Church (Second Edition). Washington, D.C.: USCCB, 1997.

Code of Canon Law (for the Latin Church). Pope John Paul II. 1983.

General Instruction of the Roman Missal (with adaptations for dioceses in the United States of America). Vatican Congregation for Divine Worship and the Discipline of the Sacraments. English translation by International Committee on English in the Liturgy. Published by the United States Conference of Catholic Bishops, 2011.

Sacrosanctum Concilium. Constitution on the Sacred Liturgy. Second Vatican Council (Pope Paul VI). December 4, 1963.

United States Catholic Catechism for Adults. Washington, D.C.: USCCB, 2006.

By Cardinal Donald Wuerl and Mike Aquilina

The Mass: The Glory, the Mystery, the Tradition. New York: Doubleday Religion, 2011.

By Cardinal Donald Wuerl

Seek First the Kingdom: Challenging the Culture by Living Our Faith. Huntington, IN: Our Sunday Visitor, 2011.

The Catholic Way: Faith for Living Today. New York: Doubleday Religion, 2001.

The Church and Her Sacraments: Making Christ Visible. Huntington, IN: Our Sunday Visitor, 1990.

The Teaching of Christ: A Catholic Catechism for Adults. Coeditor with Father Ronald Lawler, Thomas Comerford Lawler, and Father Kris Stubna. Huntington, IN: Our Sunday Visitor, 2004.

The Gift of Faith: A Question and Answer Catechism. Coauthor with Father Ronald Lawler and Thomas Comerford Lawler. Huntington, IN: Our Sunday Visitor, 2001.

The Catholic Priesthood Today. Chicago: Franciscan Herald Press, 1976.

Fathers of the Church. Boston, MA: St. Paul Editions, 1986.

By Mike Aquilina

Mothers of the Church: The Witness of Early Christian Women. Coauthor with Christopher Bailey. Huntington, IN: Our Sunday Visitor, 2012.

A Year with the Church Fathers: Patristic Wisdom for Daily Living. Charlotte, NC: Saint Benedict Press, 2010.

Roots of the Faith: From the Church Fathers to You. Ann Arbor, MI: Servant Books, 2010.

Praying the Psalms with the Early Christians. Coauthor with Christopher Bailey. Ijamsville, MD: Word Among Us, 2009.

Signs and Mysteries: Revealing Ancient Christian Symbols. Coauthor with Lea Marie Ravotti. Huntington, IN: Our Sunday Visitor, 2008.

The Mass of the Early Christians. Huntington, IN: Our Sunday Visitor, 2007.

What Catholics Believe: A Pocket Catechism. Coauthor with Father Kris Stubna. Huntington, IN: Our Sunday Visitor, 1999.

About the Authors

CARDINAL DONALD WUERL is the Archbishop of Washington, D.C., and the bestselling author of *The Catholic Way*. He is known nationally for his catechetical and teaching ministry and for his efforts on behalf of Catholic education.

MIKE AQUILINA is the author of more than twenty books, including *The Mass of the Early Christians* and *Fire of God's Love: 120 Reflections on the Eucharist*. He appears regularly on EWTN with Scott Hahn.

AN INSIGHTFUL GUIDE TO THE MOST
SACRED OF CATHOLIC PRACTICES

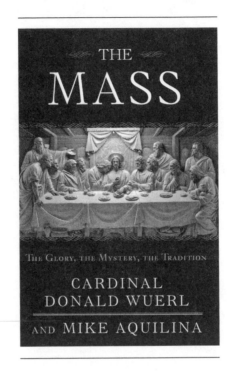

Though the Mass is at the center of Catholic life, even
the most devout can miss the rich history and spiritual
significance of its many parts. This eloquently worded
book with beautiful black-and-white illustrations
will connect modern audiences with the
meaning behind the Mass.

HARDCOVER | ISBN 978-0-307-71880-8 | $21.99 (CANADA: $24.99)
TRADE PAPERBACK | ISBN 978-0-307-71881-5 | $14.00 (CANADA: $17.00)
EBOOK | ISBN 978-0-307-71882-2 | $11.99 (CANADA: $12.99)